A River Which Sweeps Me Along

The Visual & Spiritual Imagery of Flowing Waters

A River Which Sweeps Me Along

The Visual & Spiritual Imagery of Flowing Waters

by

Arthur Gurmankin

All Photographs & Artwork

by

Arthur Gurmankin & Mary Morina

Text, Layout & Book Design by Arthur Gurmankin

•

A River Which Sweeps Me Along - ISBN 978-0-6151-6975-0

Library of Congress Control Number: 2007906998

•

A River Which Sweeps Me Along

The Visual & Spiritual Imagery of Flowing Waters

by Arthur Gurmankin

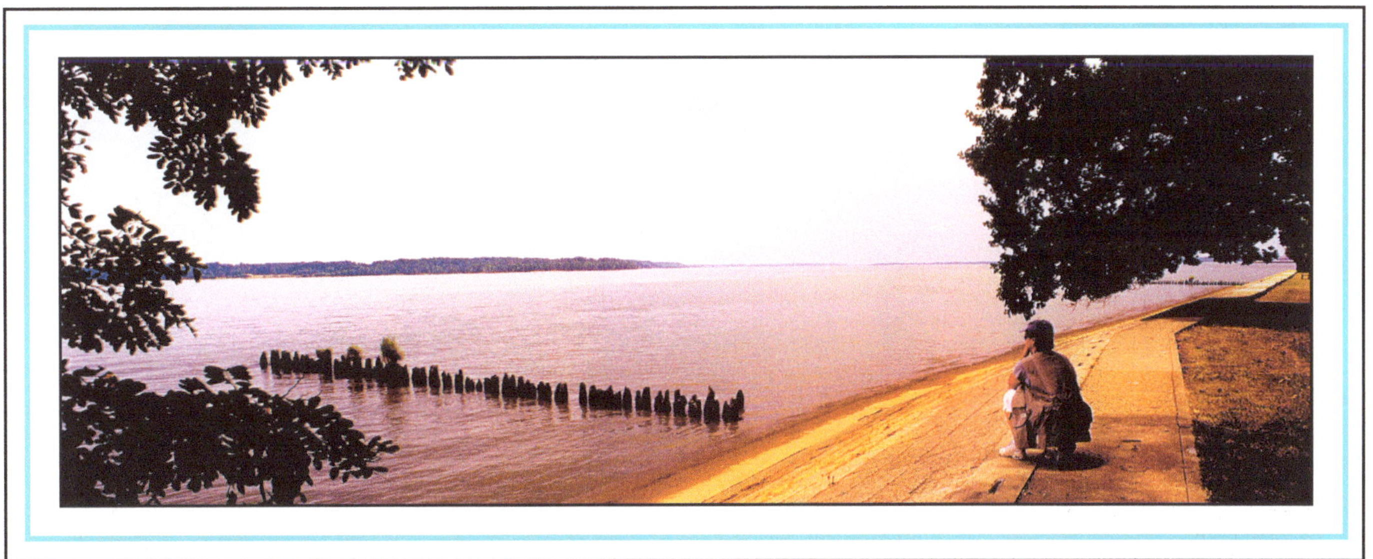

"Time is a river which sweeps me along..."

—Jorge Luis Borges

Dedicated to Chase and Erika

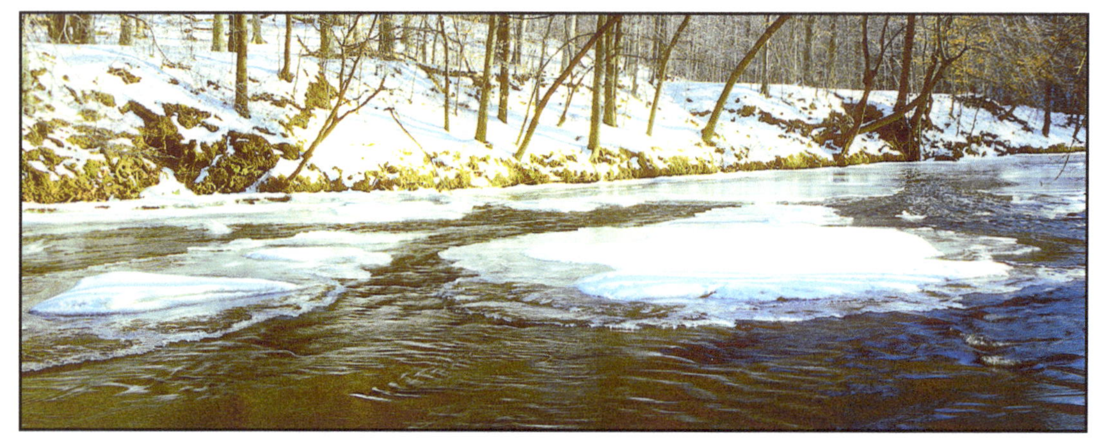

I hope you will see a time,
when all the rivers on earth flow clean and clear.

_Dude

Introduction

"Time is a river which sweeps me along…"

Jorge Luis Borges, author of these words, has given us a nearly-perfect metaphor for the entities of *time* and *life*. Standing by a river or stream, we are witness to a configuration of events that proceeds with a flow and a tempo.

Looking *upstream*, I can see the *future*, a floating leaf, an insect – moving in my direction, momentarily sharing my approximate latitude and longitude – then passing, flowing…literally into the *past* until eventually out-of-sight, temporarily or forever, out-of-mind. Downstream await perhaps, friends or acquaintances, though more likely strangers – who will see the floating leaf or mayfly of *my past* as *their oncoming and fleeting futures*. I'll never likely know if they are oblivious to the phenomenon we have shared – that particular continuum of time and space – or, if they too will wonder about it.

I have lived my entire life in a major, American city, Philadelphia, Pennsylvania. In its boundaries are two Rivers, the Delaware and Schuylkill and two streams, the Pennypack and Wissahickon Creeks. All of them have suffered to varying degrees, abuse and pollution; all are now "coming back." These flowing waters made me aware of their characteristic, visual beauty and inherently spiritual natures. Experiences that have come with age, success, setback, recovery, family, friends, gain and loss, for whatever reasons, cause me to gravitate to moving waters with increasing frequency. Perhaps I feel compelled, afraid I will miss something I've never seen, or, will see one more time, something I may never see again.

In this book, I share with you, through images and words, some of the rivers, streams, creeks and brooks that, in their separate and distinct ways, sweep me along and make me grateful for my time on earth. I hope I've succeeded in depicting how rivers and streams visually lead our eyes inward while drawing our emotional responses outward. Because many of our rivers have been misused and abused, some of what you will see and read is *editorial commentary* for which I do not in any way apologize.

Arthur Gurmankin — September, 2007

"All streams are but tributary to the ocean, which itself does not stream, and the shores are unchanged, but in longer periods than man can measure. Go where we will, we discover infinite change in particulars only, not in generals."

_Henry David Thoreau

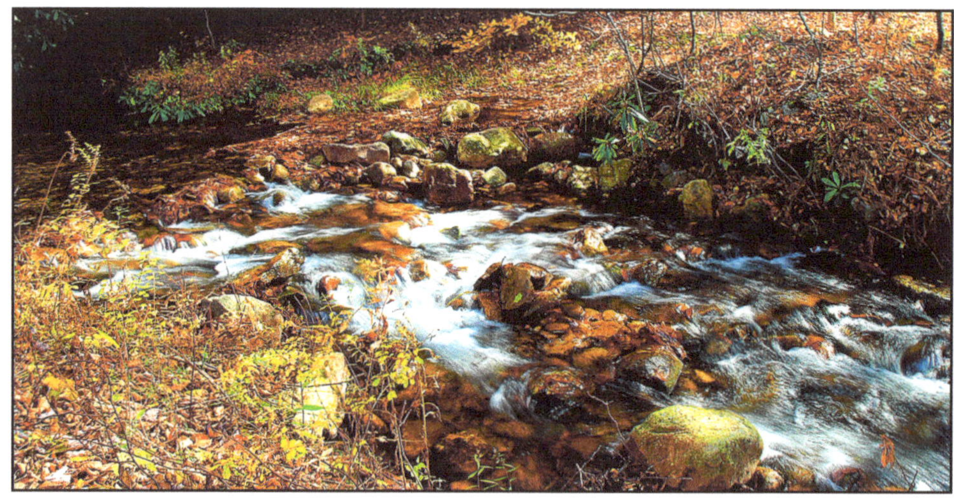

Depending on where you live, bodies of flowing water are referred to as *streams*, *rivers*, *creeks*, *brooks* and *tributaries* – often interchangeably. This "feeder" stream flows into a larger stream which in turn, flows into a river which flows into a larger river. The whole configuration, analagous in some ways to capillaries and arteries in the body, flows eventually into the Mid-Atlantic Ocean, ultimately evaporates into the atmosphere, returns to the earth's surface as some form of precipitation and sooner or later, is once again back in a tributary, etc. .

"...for movement and rhythm are of the essence of all things loveable...and every living thing is like the river, which, if it did not flow out, would never have been able to flow in."

_Alan W. Watts

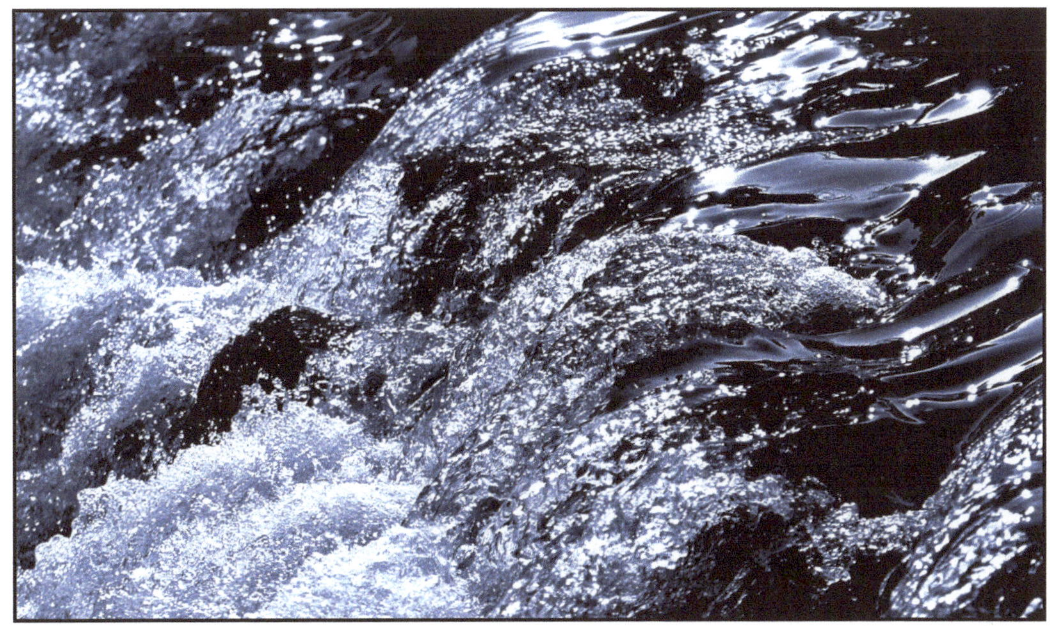

"A fine stream, fed by rivulets and mountain springs, pours through the valley."
_Washington Irving

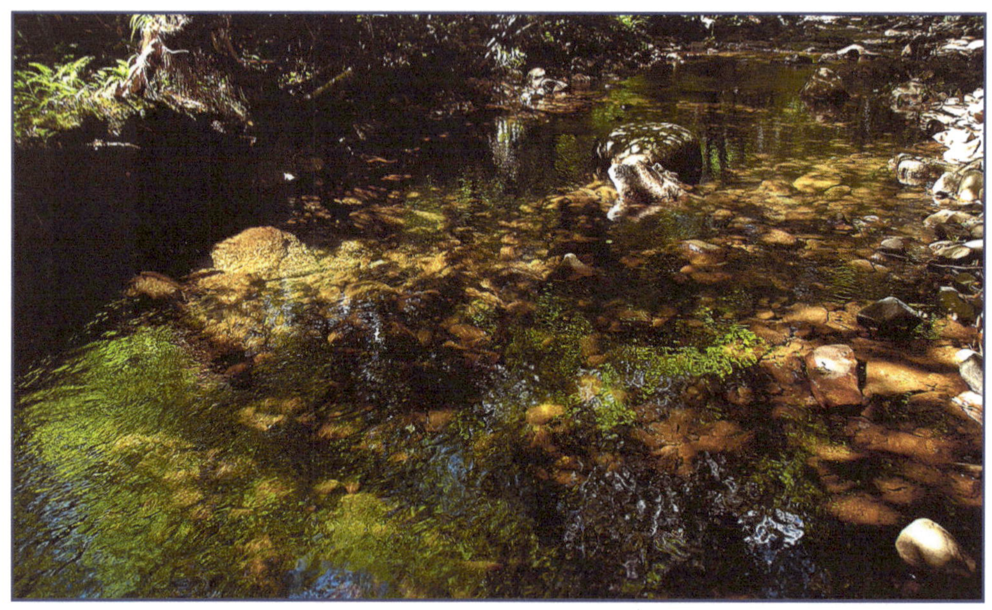

Rivers and streams are the designers and architects that sweep and move the earth. Of all the forces that shape land-masses, flowing water is the most wide-ranging and dramatic. Broad rivers, small streams, even relatively short-lived runoffs, over time find the earth's paths of least resistance (which are sometimes made of rock). Stream beds (channels) may stay relatively straight, or meander, as flowing waters transporting sediments, pebbles, rocks and other debris, widen and deepen them.

"The 'control of nature' is a phrase conceived in arrogance..."

_Rachel Carson

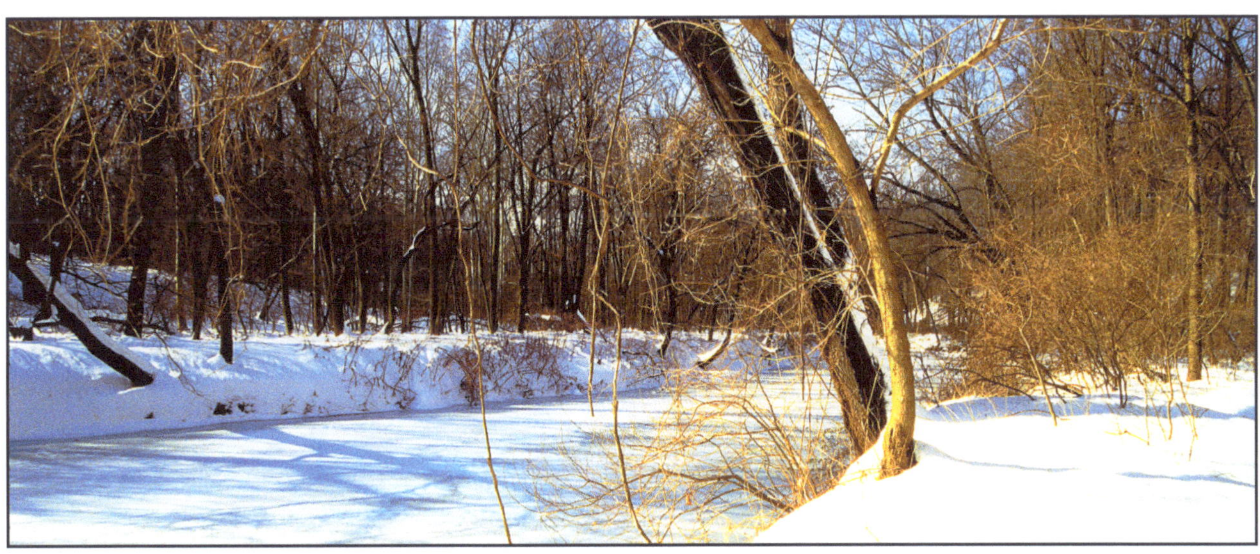

All rivers and streams flow in *one* direction – *downhill.* Depending on the gradient or downward slope and the composition of the land it traverses, the velocity of the flow will vary. Evaporation, freezing, precipitation and the absortion of water by plants or the ground, contribute to fluctuations in depths. Flowing waters are bound to certain inevitabilities…as are our lives.

"...we have been as usual asking the wrong question. It does not matter a hoot what the mockingbird on the chimney is singing....The real and proper question is: Why is it beautiful?"

_Annie Dillard

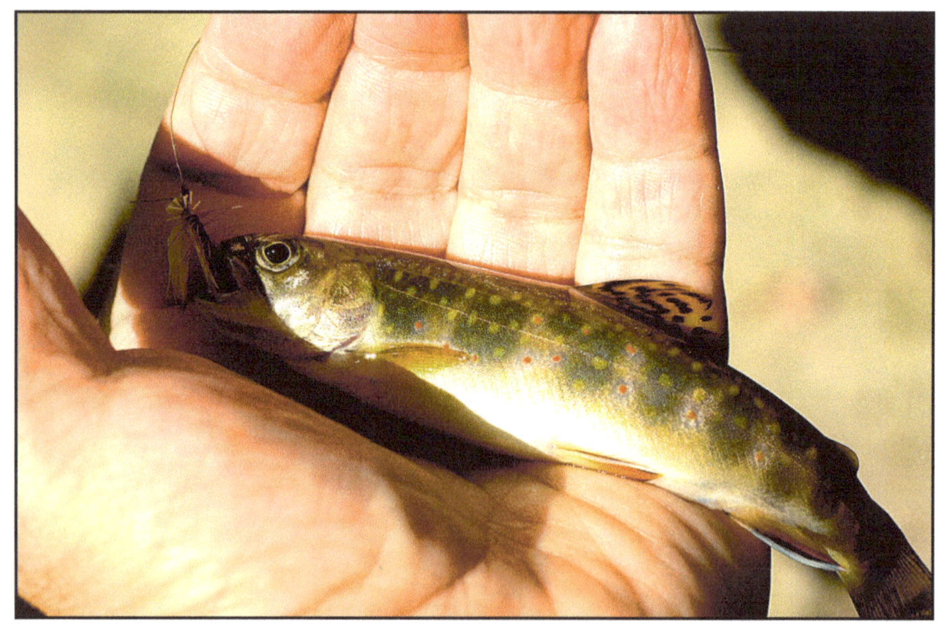

I took his picture then put him back...as always. The Brook Trout is one of the most beautiful creatures on earth. It requires clean streams and rivers to survive. A favorite of flyfishermen, the more enlightened ones practice what is known as "catch and release," using artificial "flies" with barbless hooks. The poet Joyce Kilmer wrote "...only God can make a tree," to which I add, "...or a brook trout."

"Beside a stream, don't waste water; even in a forest, don't waste fire wood."
_Chinese Proverb

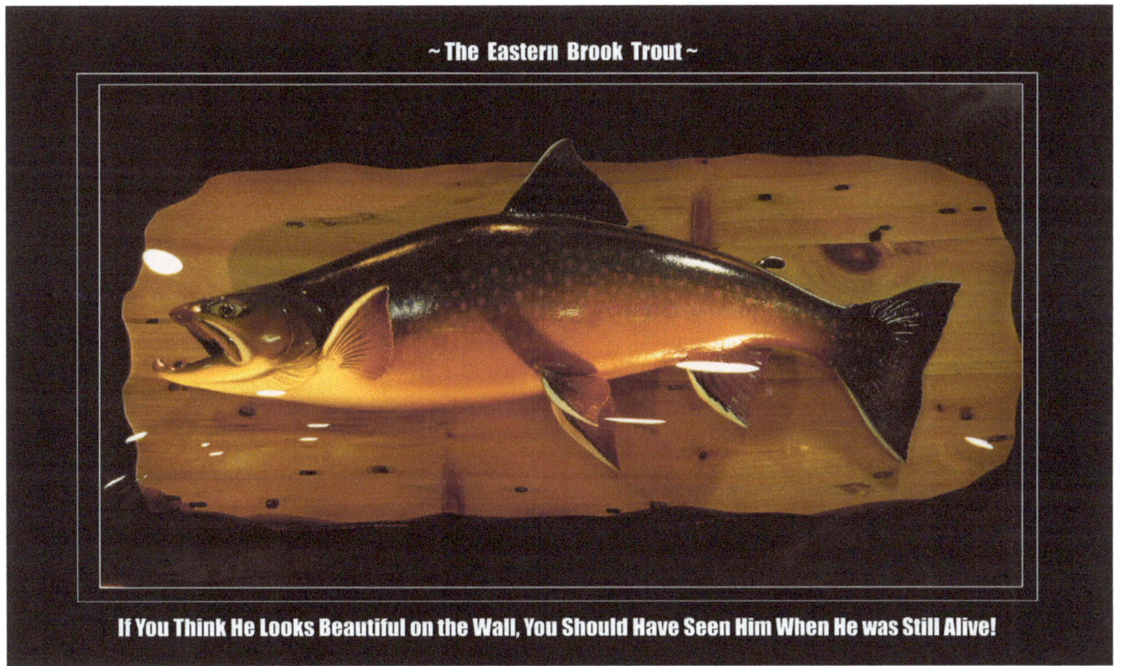

The actions of man are frequently careless, self-serving, egotistical and destructive. Fortunately, there are private and public entities working to conserve, preserve, restore and enhance rivers and streams. Unfortunately, there are also entities working to develop land near streams and exploit them for personal gain.

In recent years, technologies have emerged to allow replicas to be made of fish caught, photographed and released unharmed. This takes ego out of the equation and preserves the resource.

As the saying goes, "We all live downstream."

"Smooth runs the water where the brook is deep."

_William Shakespeare

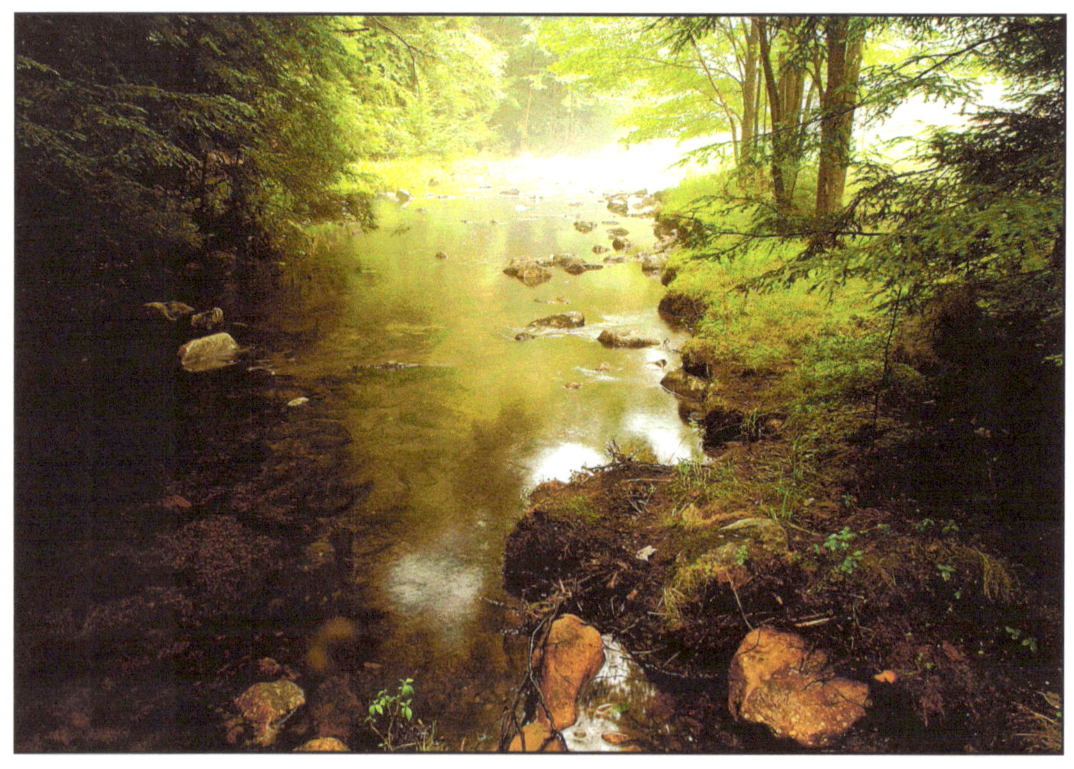

"Eventually, all things merge into one, and a river runs through it."

__Norman MacLean

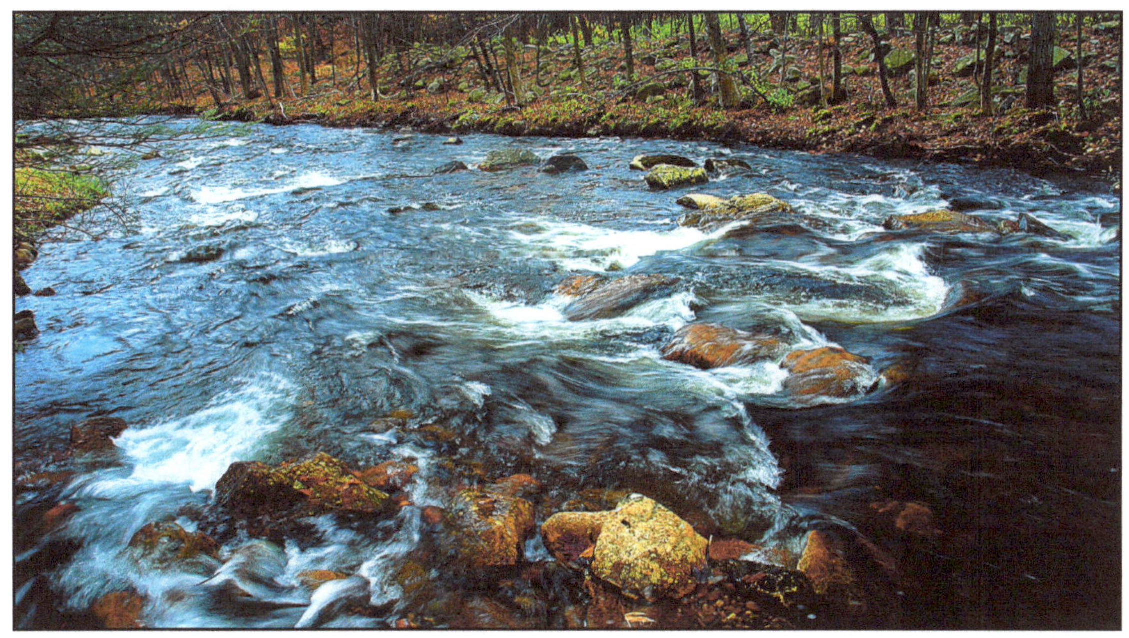

No ecosystem exists, nor can it be studied or understood in isolation, just as our personal histories could not be written omitting references to what we've experienced to any given moment in time. River and stream environments are no exception; all of the living and non-living components in, around, below and above a river, together make it both similar to, and different from, all others.

"Water doesn't flow if it's level, and people won't complain if you treat them on the level."
_Chinese proverb.

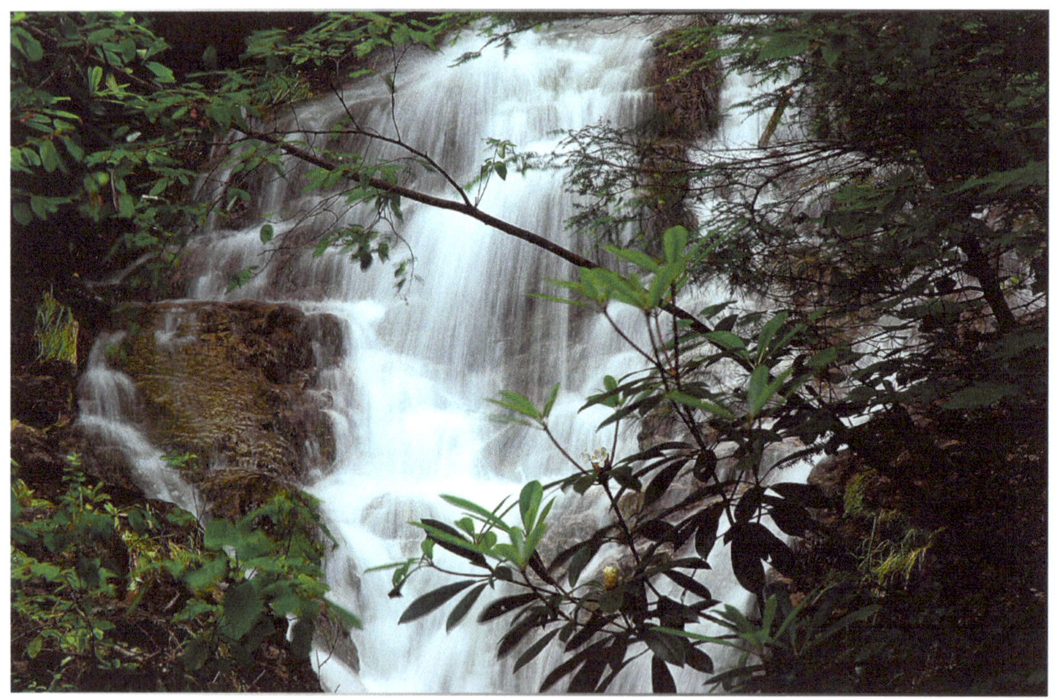

Streams flowing over more-or-less flat terrain, *meander* from side-to-side. Geographer Anne Chin, Texas A&M University, was likely first to identify that *mountain streams* also meander, but *vertically*, "dropping from pool to pool at a rhythmic, periodic rate." Thus a mountain stream can be compared to a sequence of staircase-like patterns.

*"A river seems a magic thing. A magic, moving, living part of the very earth itself—
for it is from the soil, both from its depth and from its surface, that a river has its beginning."*
_Laura Gilpin, U.S. Photographer

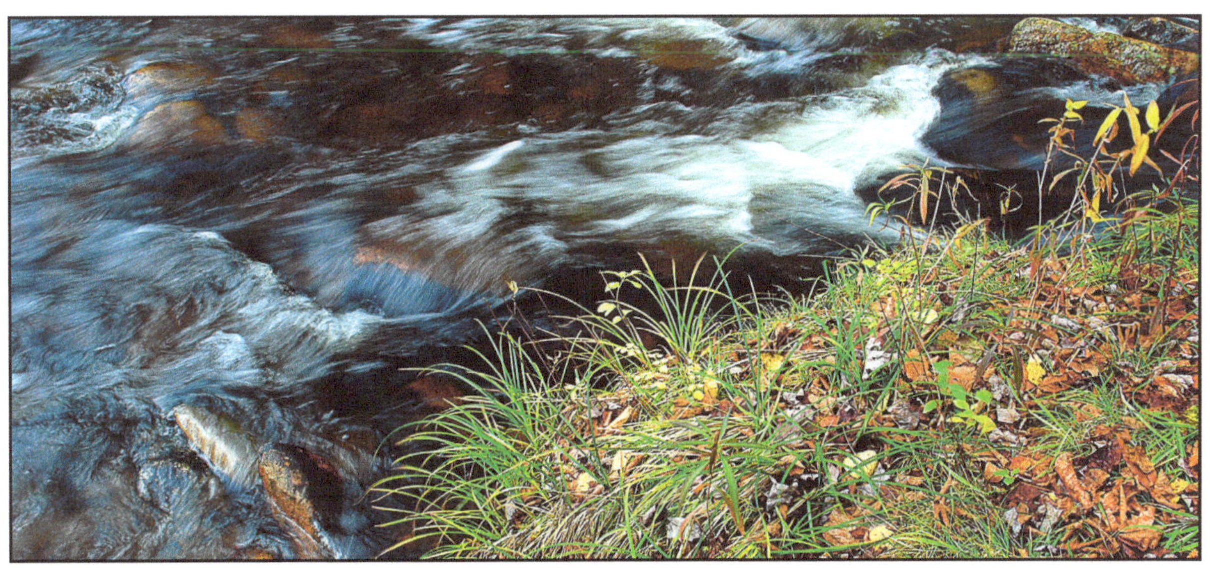

"The river knows the way to the sea;
Without a pilot it runs and falls, Blessing all lands with its charity."

__Ralph Waldo Emerson

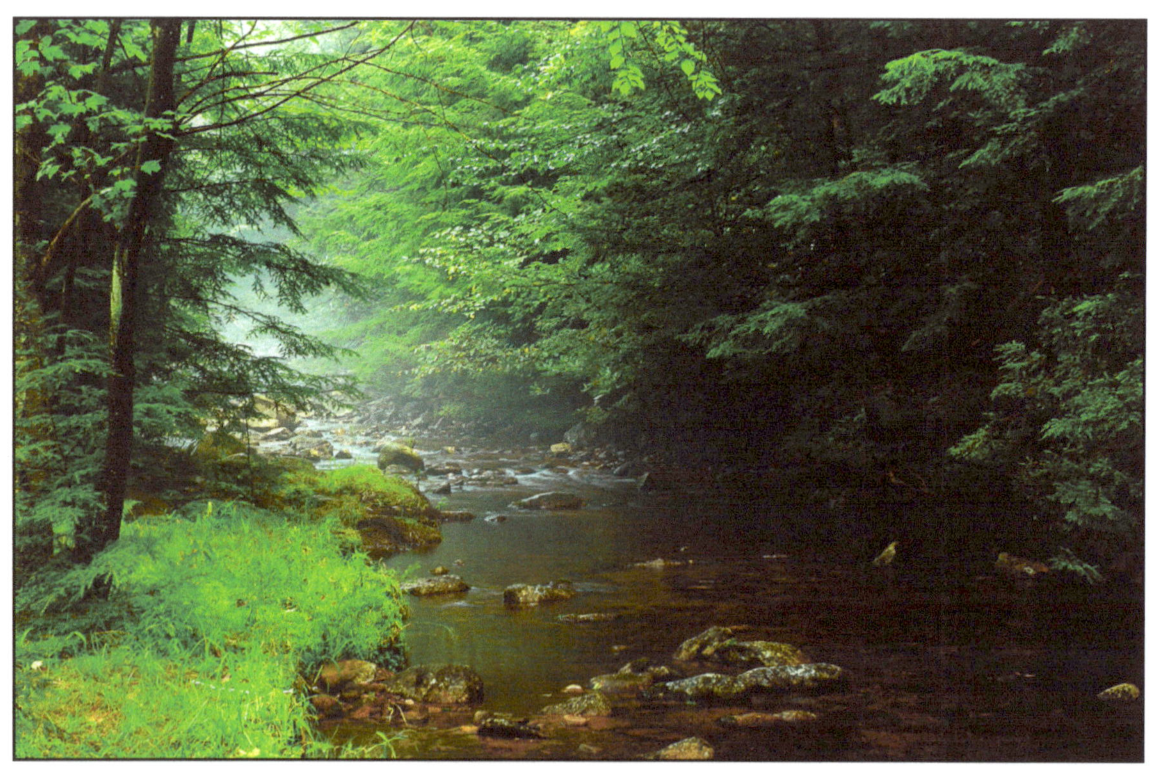

"The movement of change is as much the builder as the destroyer."
_Alan W. Watts

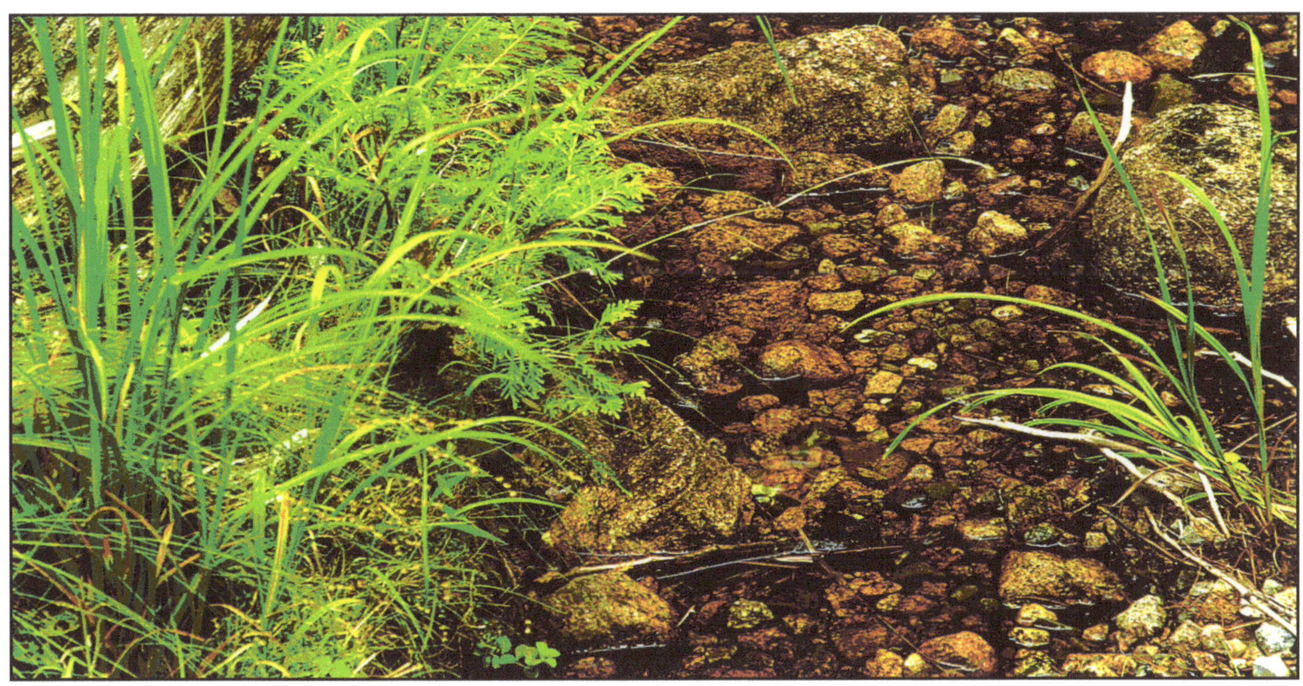

Erosion is the process that gradually wears away land; glaciers, temperature changes, waves, ice, wind and running water dissolve, fragment, pick up and carry soil and rock from one location to another. The rocks and pebbles in this brook's bed (or channel) have been worn away over thousands of years. their fragments deposited elsewhere transported as silt, sand, mud or even boulders.

"Trickling water, if not stopped, will become a mighty river."
_Chinese proverb. Confucius.

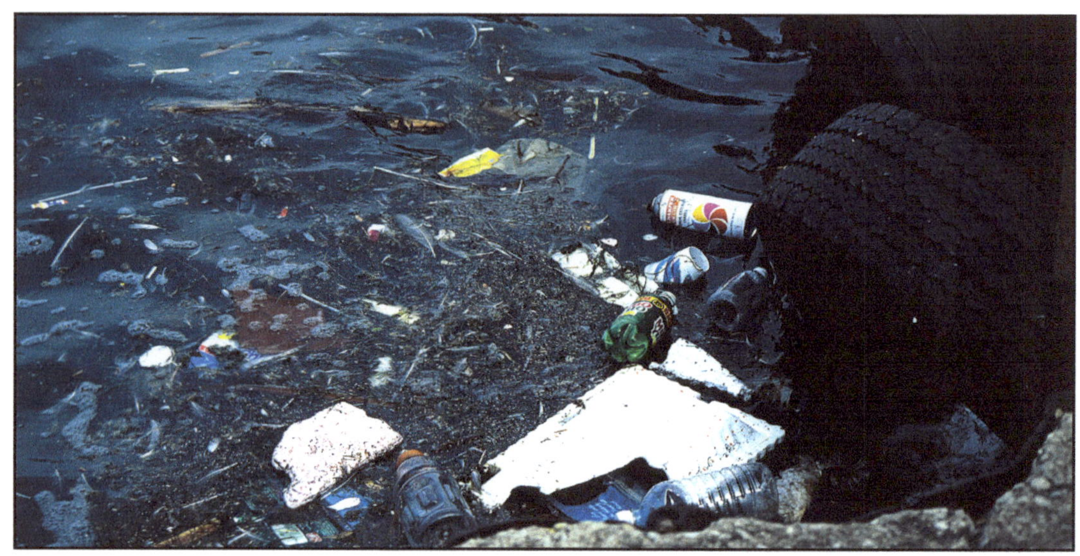

Ever heard the term "Urban Runoff?" After land is cleared, developers move in and cover drainage areas with buildings and concrete. As a result, oil, fertilizer, weed and insect killers – *pollutants,* along with trash and garbage – run directly into streams at increasing rates. Sewage systems can fail and spill their contents which also ends up in rivers. Treated sewage too gets discharged directly into the rivers and disrupts ecological balance; harmful chemicals build up in fish and other food organisms and subsequently poison humans and wildlife.

In the manufacturing process, even certain prescription medications such as anti-depressants, become contaminated.

Drip, drip, drip.

*"When a sparrow sips in the river, the water doesn't recede.
Giving charity does not deplete wealth."*

_Punjabi proverb

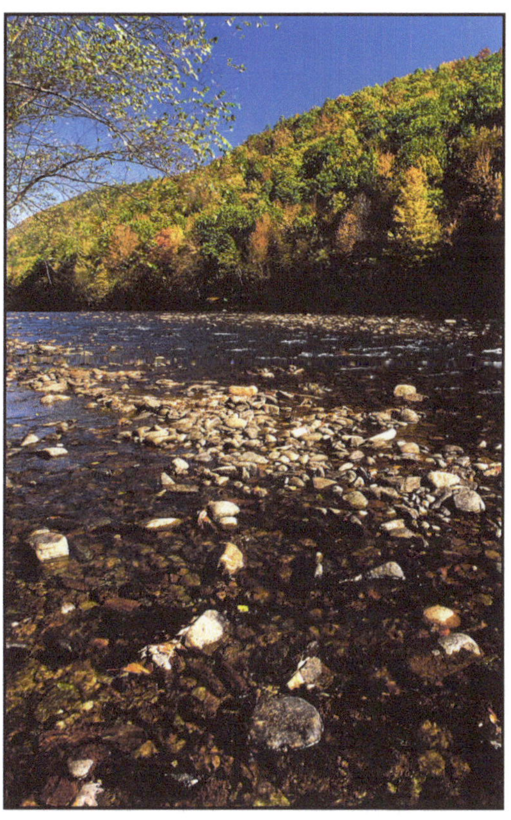

Vanishing streams? In many areas of the U.S. water comes mainly from wells. As populations increase, more water is taken from the ground (water tables) so levels fall. Wells are drilled deeper, springs and aquifers dry up as do streams and rivers. Most of us fail to make a connection between ground water and river water but the result is the same as if water was being drained directly from the river. Legislators who give in to lobbies pushing for increased development, likely know the potential environmental impact; but they also likely know that sapping water from *beneath* a river is way around conservation laws.

*"Shall we gather at the river, Where bright angel feet have trod;
With its crystal tide for ever, Flowing by the throne of God?"*

_Robert Lowry

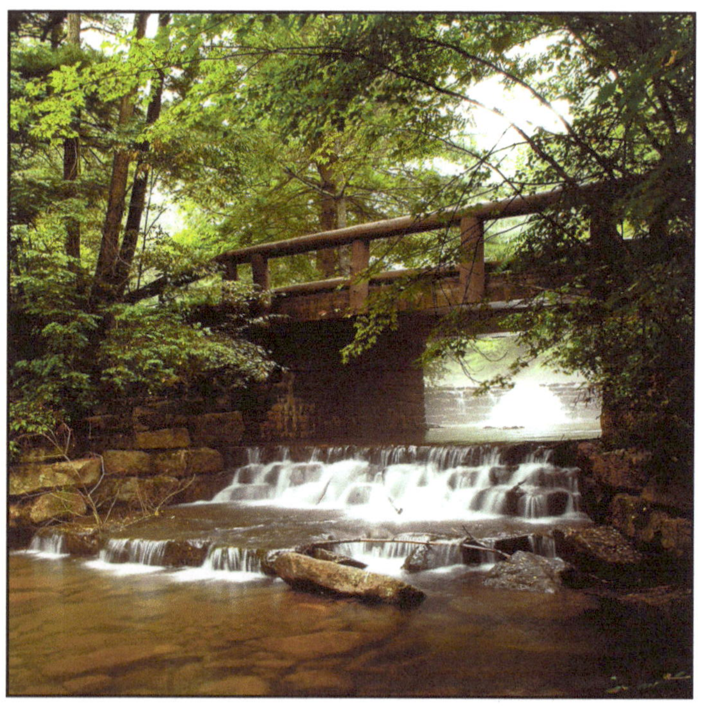

Even in conjunction with made-made structures, a river or stream can create a sense of spirituality. Thankfully, there are artists, designers, environmentalists and engineers who work cooperatively to create harmonious unions between nature and civilization.

"It is impossible to step into the same river twice."

_Heraclitus (Greek philosopher)

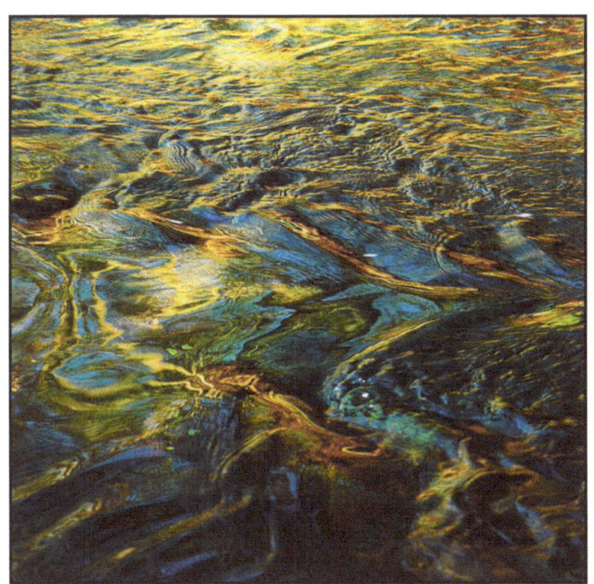

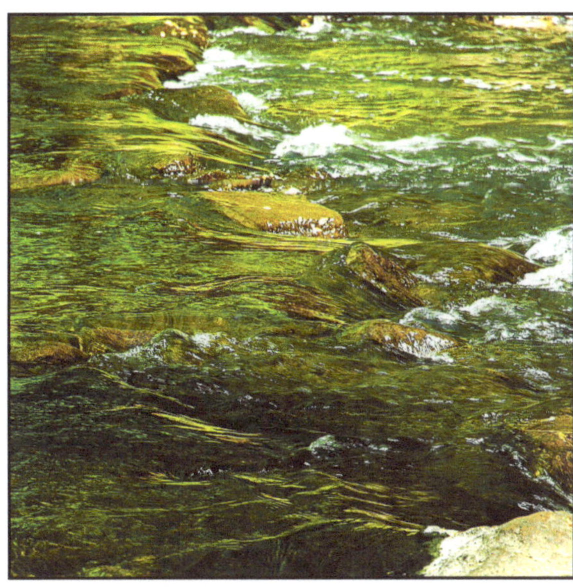

These two images are of virtually the same portion of the same stream; they were taken at different times of the day and year with different water levels and clarity conditions. Every moment in time and space differs in some ways from every other.

"I was born upon thy bank, river, My blood flows in thy stream,
And thou meanderest forever, At the bottom of my dream."

_Henry David Thoreau

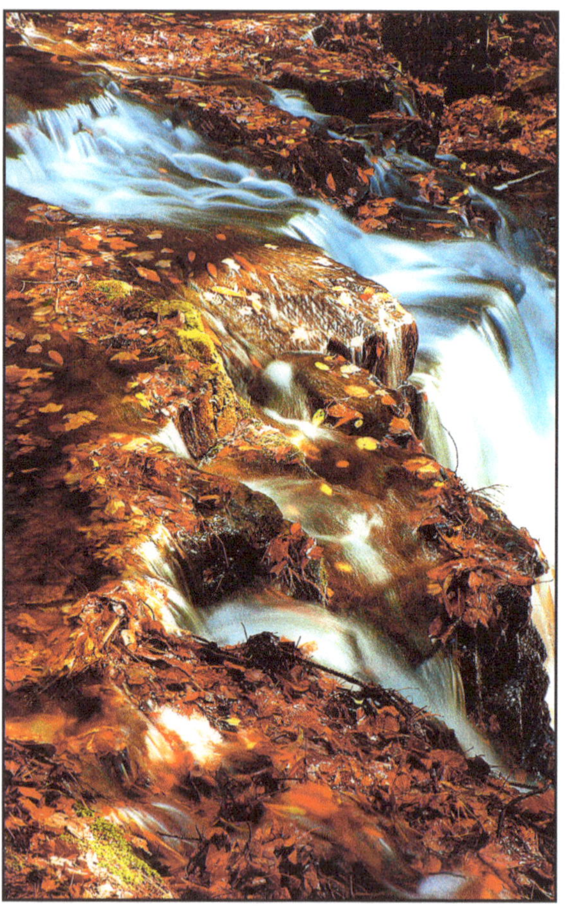

Perhaps one of many cosmic prototypes, a river or stream is analogous to the circulatory systems of both simple and complex life forms. Pushing the comparison, a flowing stream like the flow of blood through veins, arteries and capillaries, is part of an integrated set of systems that carry a variety of useful and used-up materials in an unending recycling process.

"Man is a stream whose source is hidden.
Our being is descending into us from we know not whence."
_Ralph Waldo Emerson

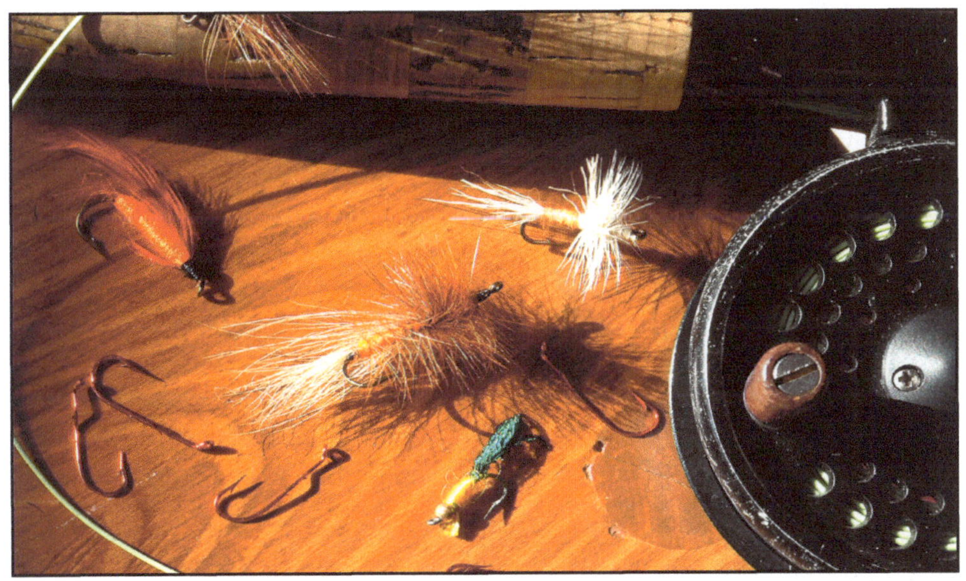

Typically, a valley that's beneath the *water table* (the level where the ground is saturated), will have a stream fed by that ground water in the form of *springs*. These so-called "spring creeks" mantain fairly constant water temperature year round. They are also often in proximity to limestone veins thus making them rich in mineral content. These two factors, while essentially the manifestations of *hidden* phenomena, are, among other things, a trout fisherman's dream.

"Time is but the stream I go a-fishing in".

_Henry David Thoreau

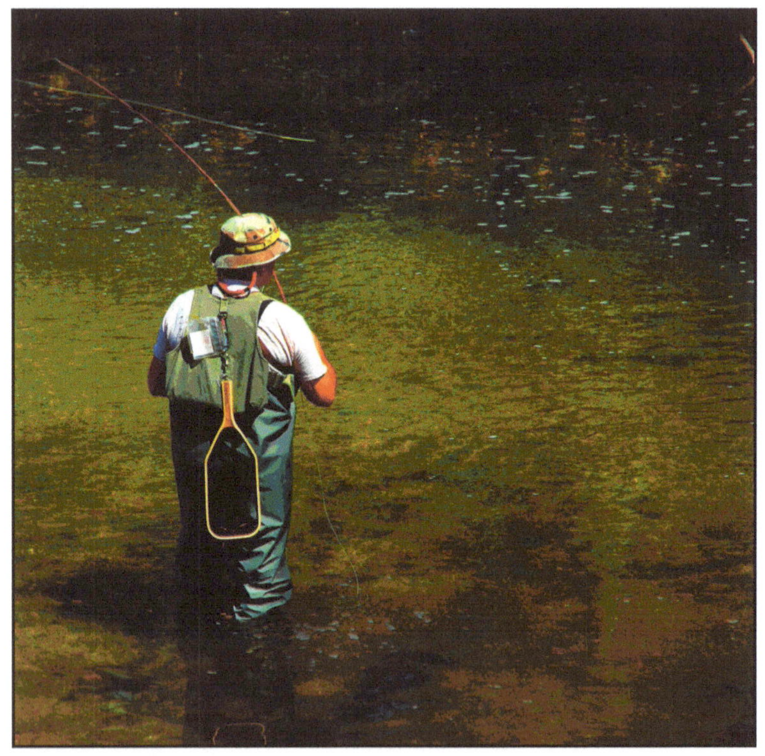

Many fishermen with whom I've spoken and a number of authors I've read, agree that the appeal of fishing is not so much in the *catching* as in the mystery and anticipation of what might come out of the water with the next cast and the next. So it is – we *bide our time*, *go with the flow* or *try to swim against the current.*

*"The creeks ... are an active mystery, fresh every minute.
Theirs is the mystery of continuous creation and all that providence implies..."*

__Annie Dillard

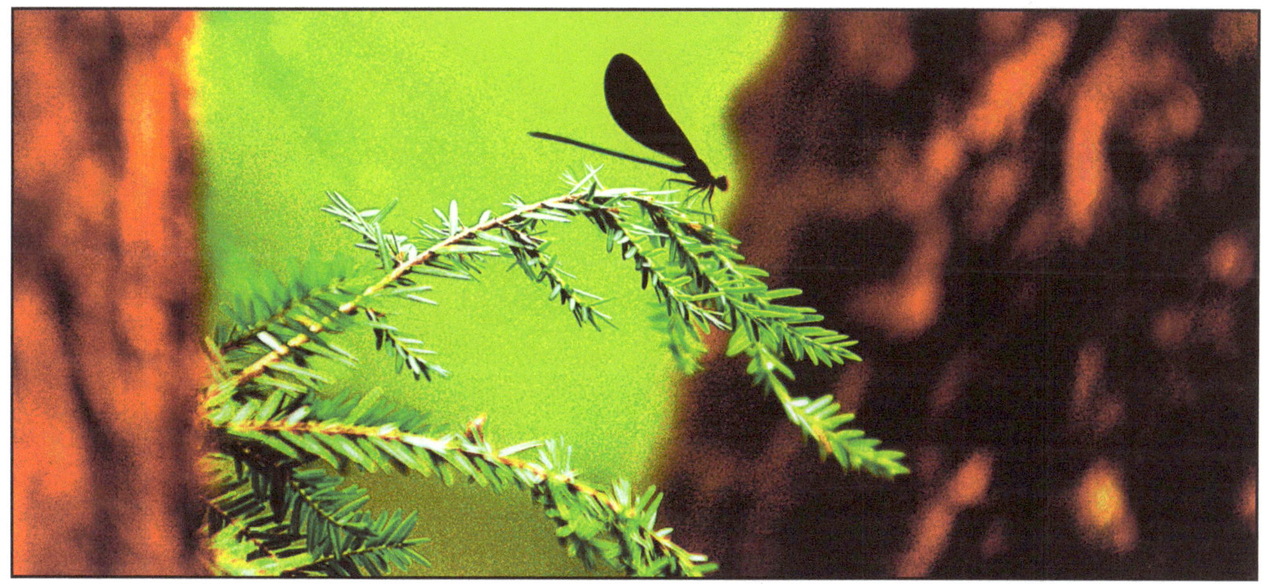

Insects like the Black-winged Damselfly and a multitude of other organisms, are sustained by slow-moving streams. Females deposit eggs, one-at-a-time into soft-stemmed aquatic plants, the perfect incubators – food is comprised mainly of small aquatic insects, perfectly provided to help assure a future.

Plants and animals of stream/creek/brook/river ecosystems, occupy their respective *ecological niches* linked to living and non-living components which together form a complex unit, simultaneously dynamic and constant.

*"...he died as the mist rises from the brook, which the sun will soon dart his rays through.
Do not the flowers die every autumn?
Soon the note of the lark will be heard down in the meadow,
and fresh dandelions will spring from the old stocks where he plucked them last summer."*

_Henry David Thoreau

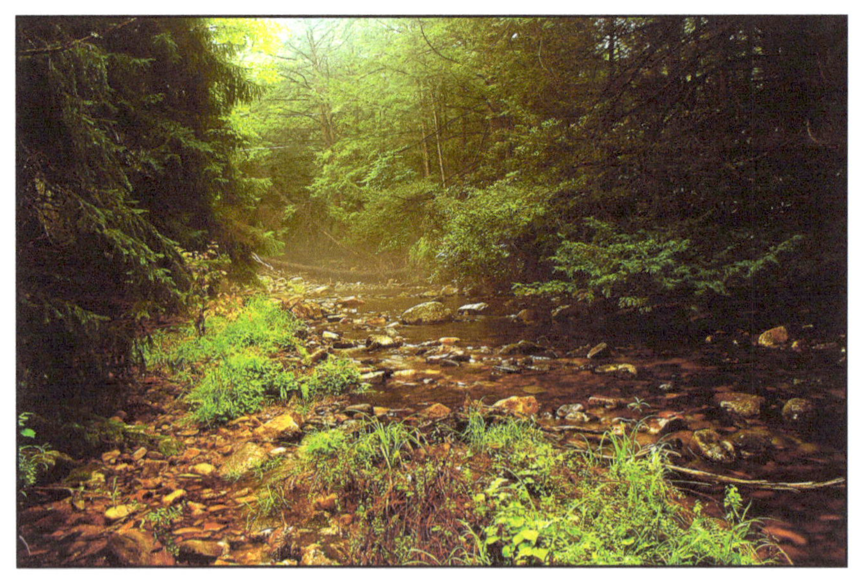

"Memory is a net; one finds it full of fish when he takes it from the brook; but a dozen miles of water have run through it without sticking."

_Oliver Wendell Holmes, Sr.

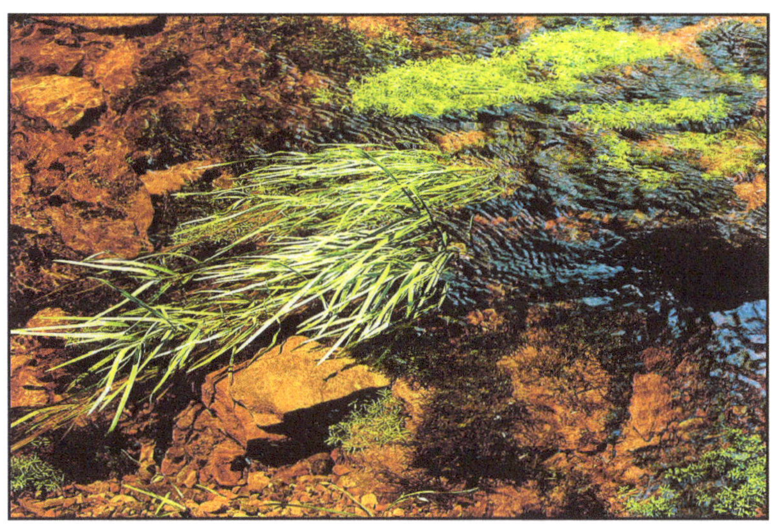

Plants rooted in the beds of spring-fed streams manifest the water current's direction, undulation and rhythm while remaining essentially in the same location. Our minds are capable of being *opened*, *closed* or *selective*, this while standing constantly in the midst of a stream-of-consciousness or some variation on that theme.

"Speaking of contraries, see how the brook
In that white wave runs counter to itself.
It is from that in water we were from
Long, long before we were from any creature."

_Robert Frost

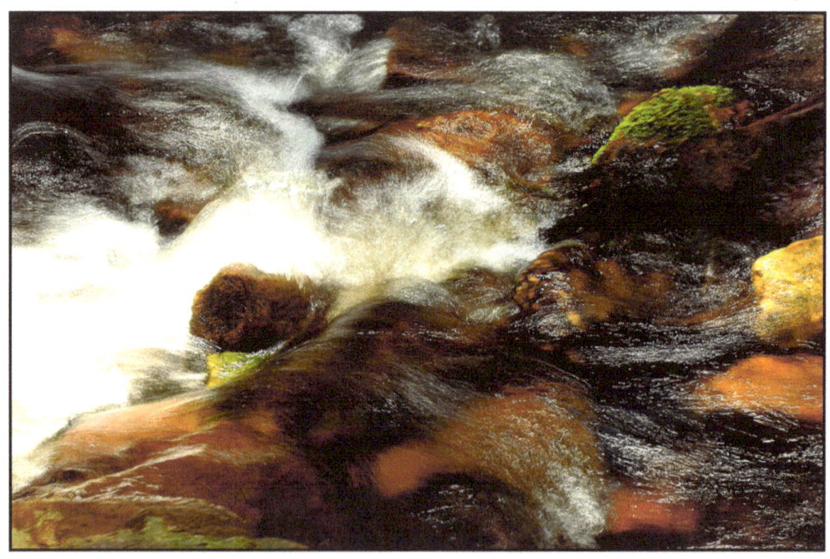

No concept can be fully understood without its opposite; if we never saw *black*, would we recognize *white*? Where would *up* be without *down*? And if we'd never encountered a rainy night in the Month of November, wouldn't a perfect, sunny day in May, be somehow diminished?

"Water's my will, and my way, and the spirit runs, intermittently,
In and out of the small waves…"

_Theodore Roethke

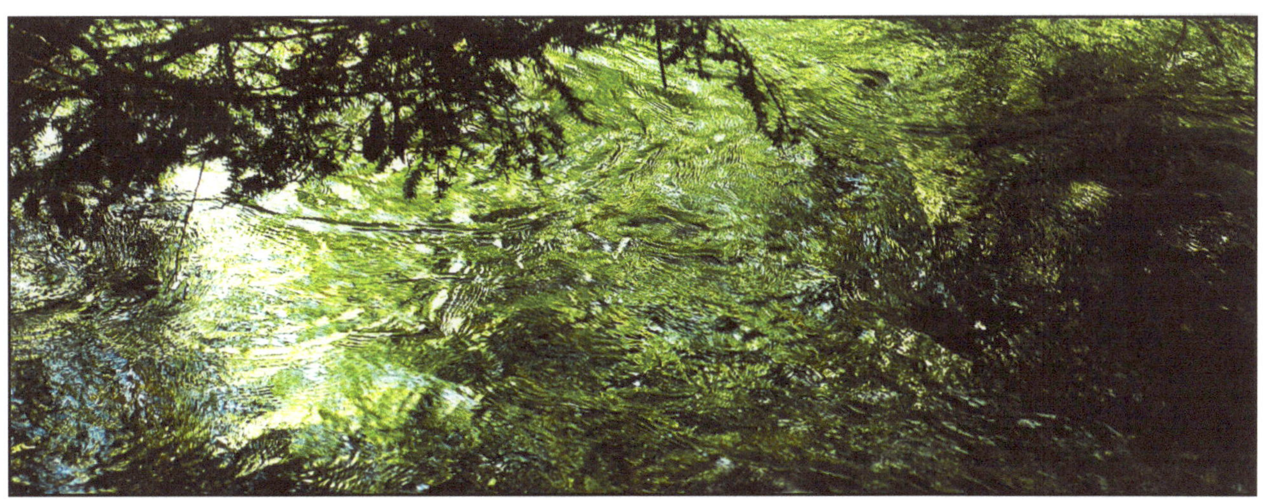

"If water is too clear, it will not contain fish;
people who are too cautious will never gain wisdom."

_Chinese proverb.

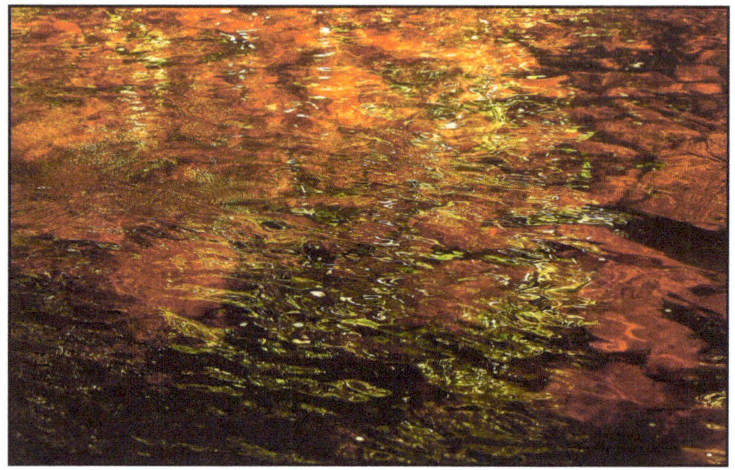

In flowing bodies of water, clear or *apparently* clear conditions are crucial to a healthy environment. Rock and gravel bottoms sustain fish and insect egg incubation; eggs settle in spaces between bottom gravel which must be free of silt and sediment lest incubating eggs can't "breathe." The bottom substrate also provides habitat for food-chain organisms.

While the most productive areas of streams and rivers are the clean-swept rocks and gravel of their pools and riffles which may well appear clear to the naked eye or casual observer, they actually teem with the essences of life.

"To everything there is a season…"
_Old Testament (Ecclesiastes iii. 1)

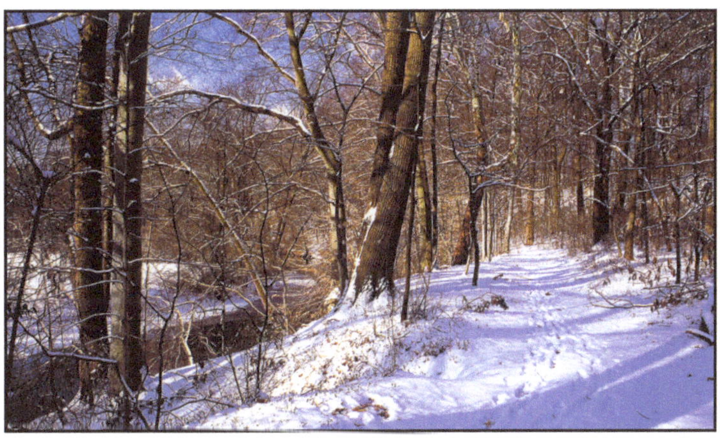

Winter

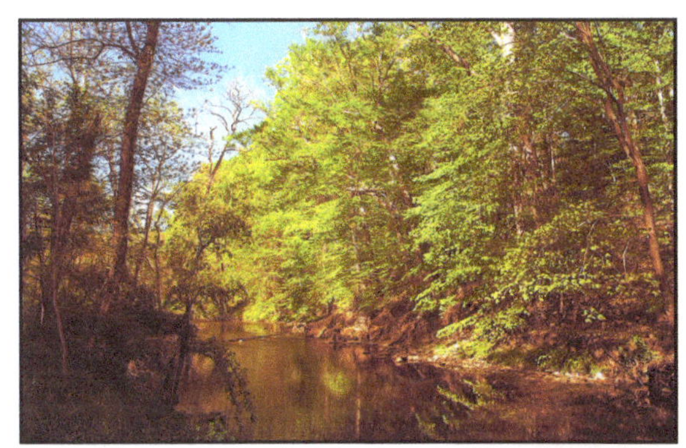

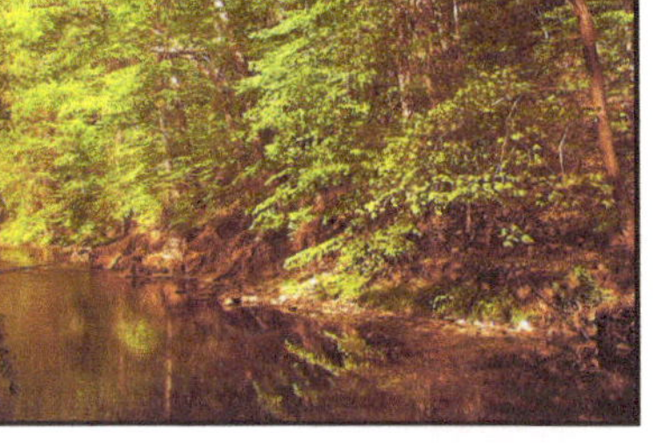

Spring

Summer

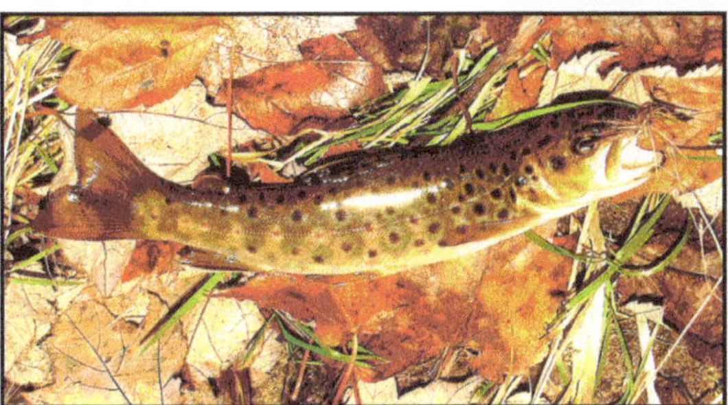

Autumn

Winter

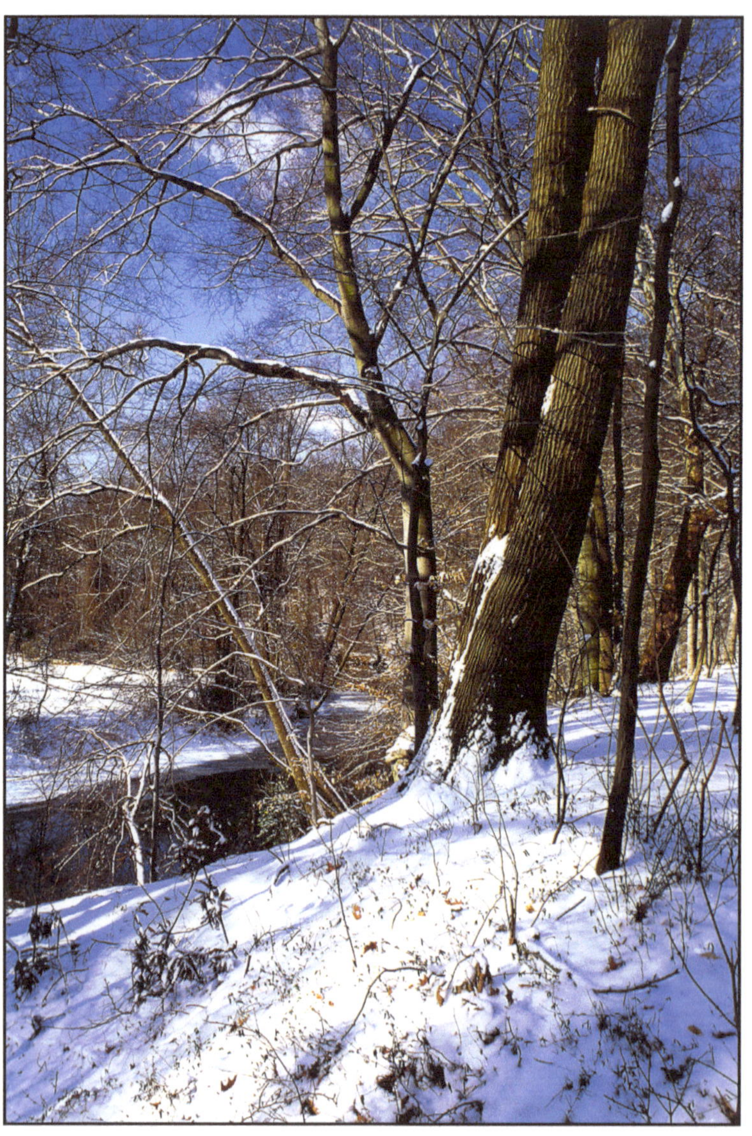

Winter

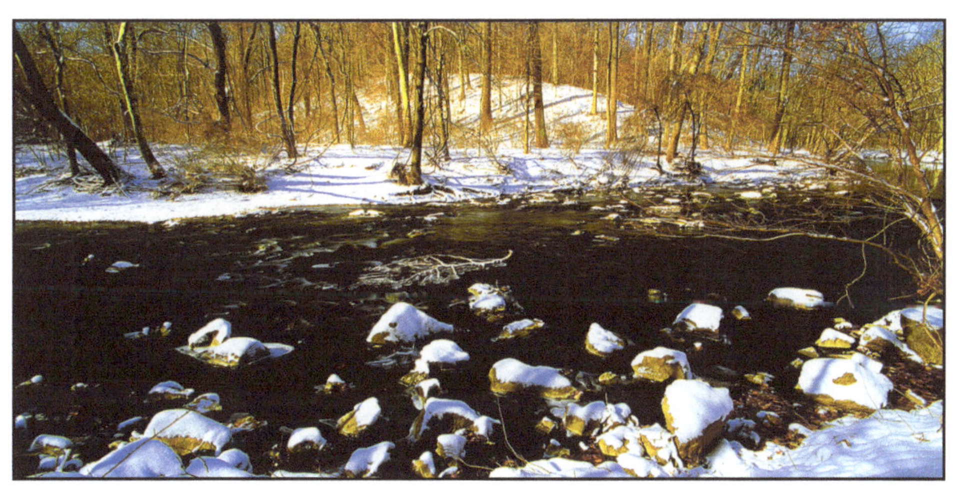

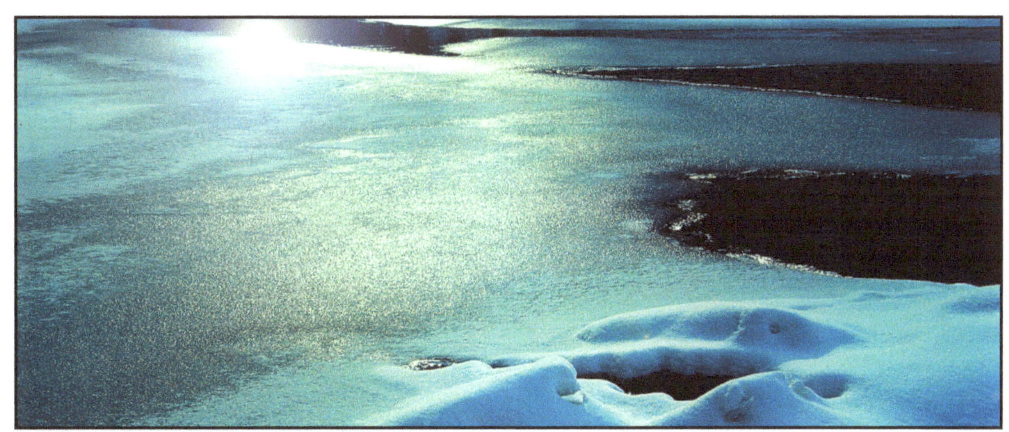

Spring

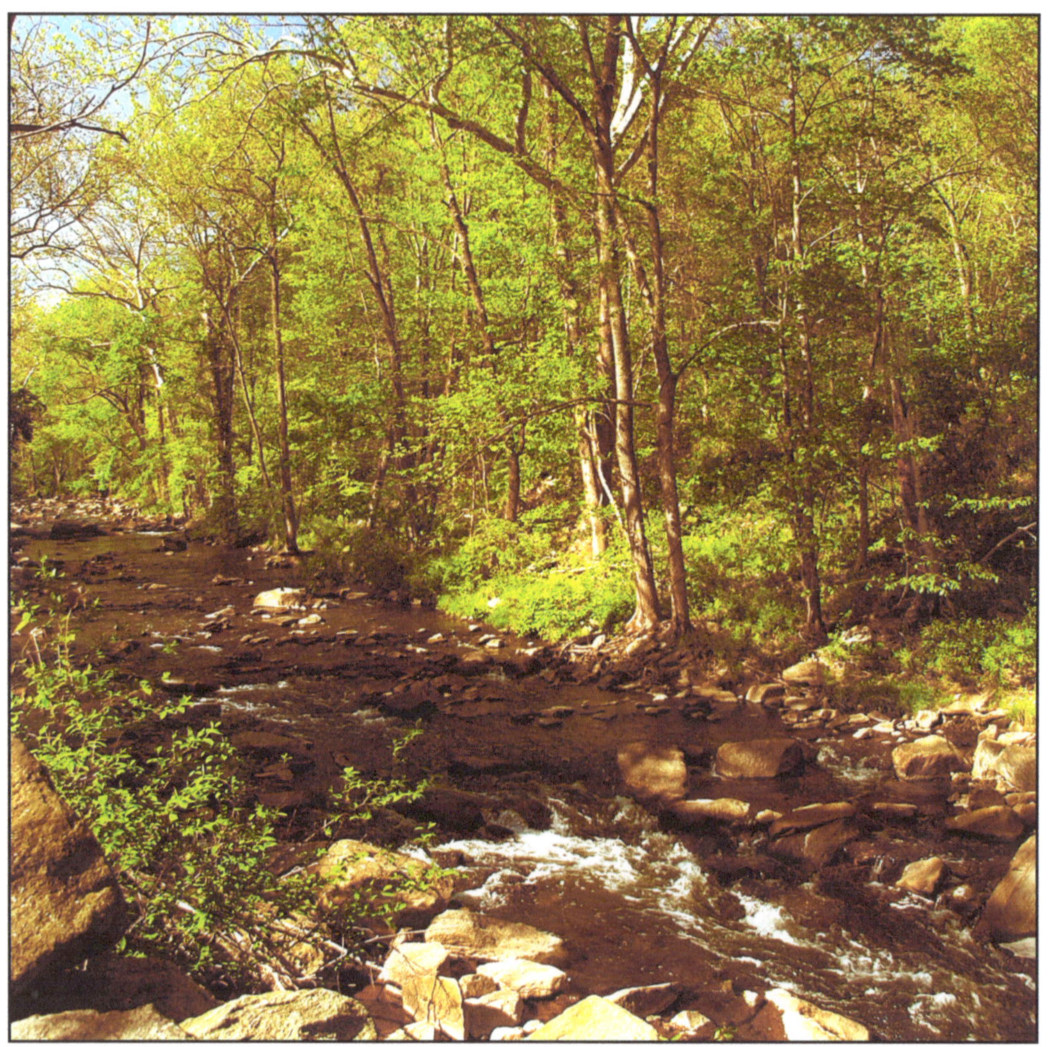

Spring

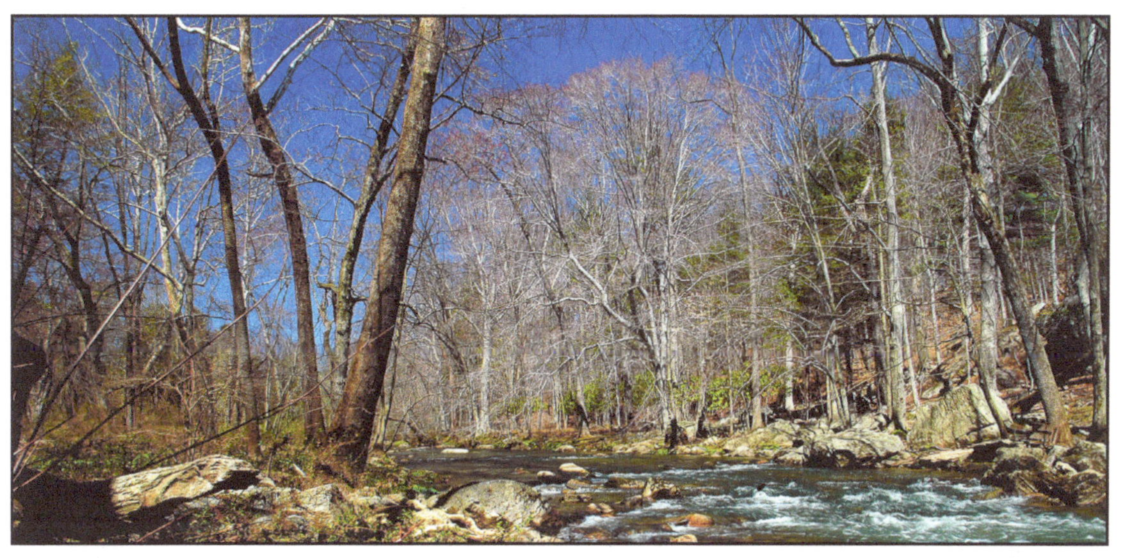

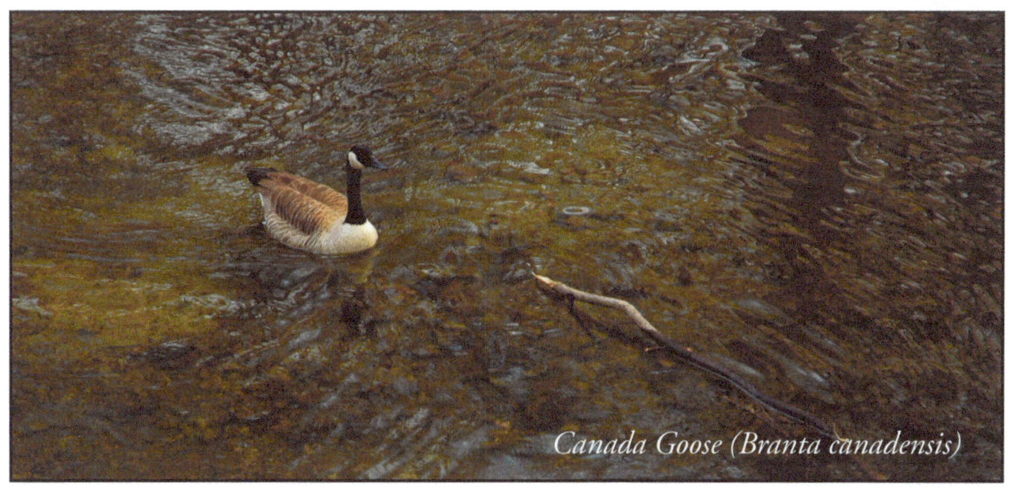

Canada Goose (Branta canadensis)

Summer

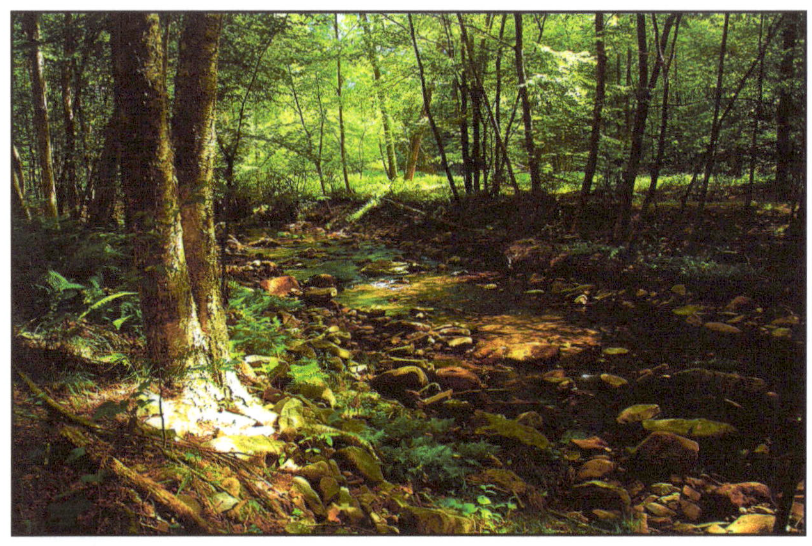

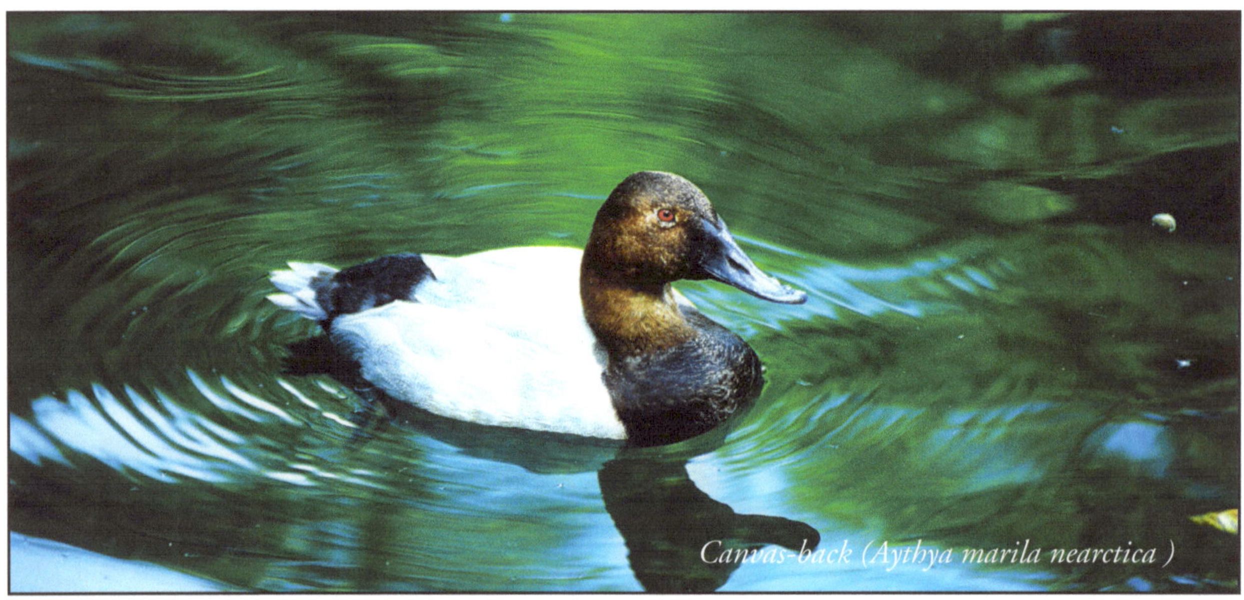

Canvas-back (Aythya marila nearctica)

Summer

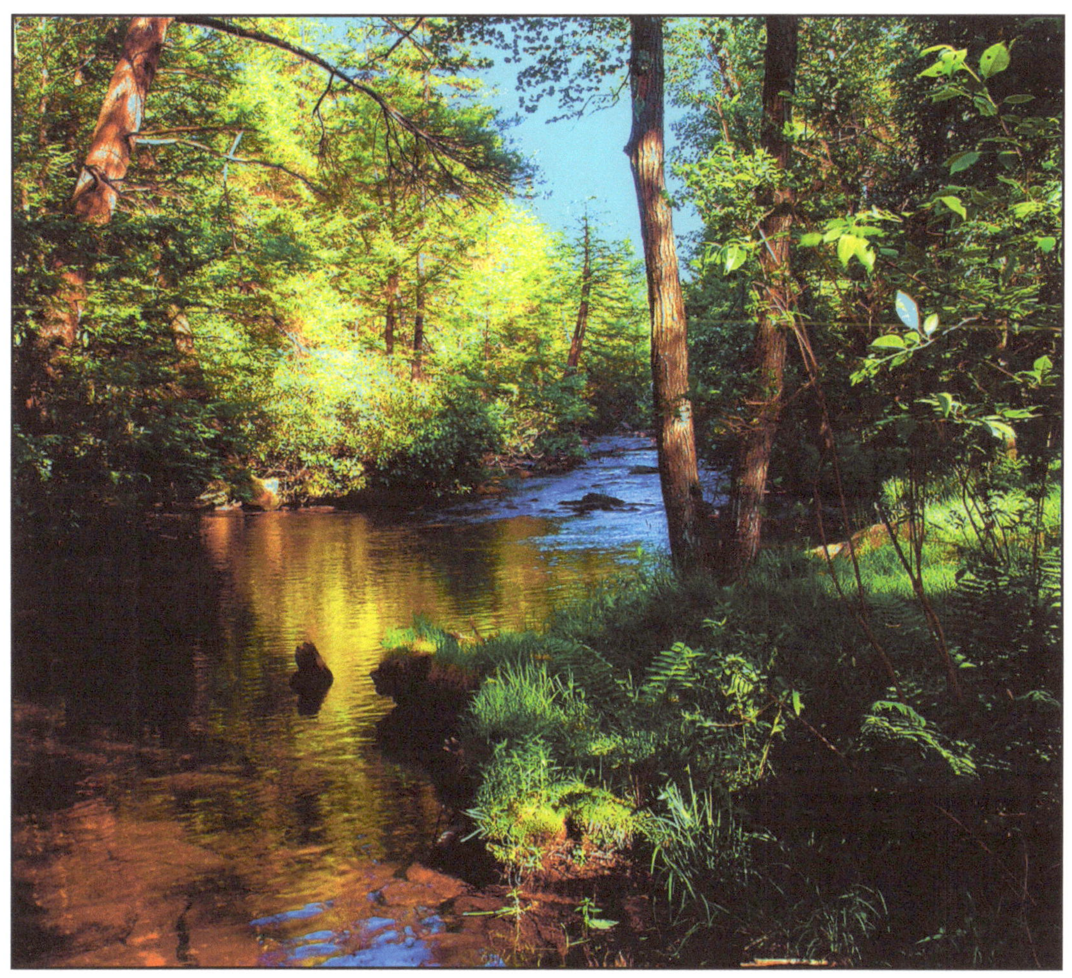

Autumn

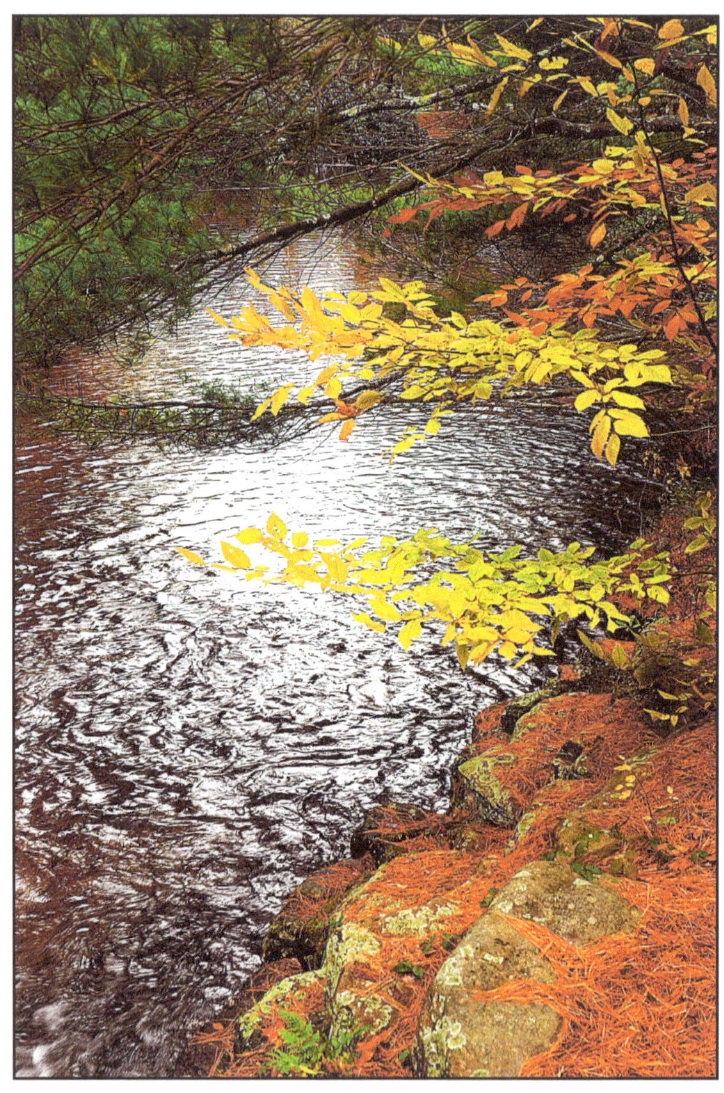

Autumn

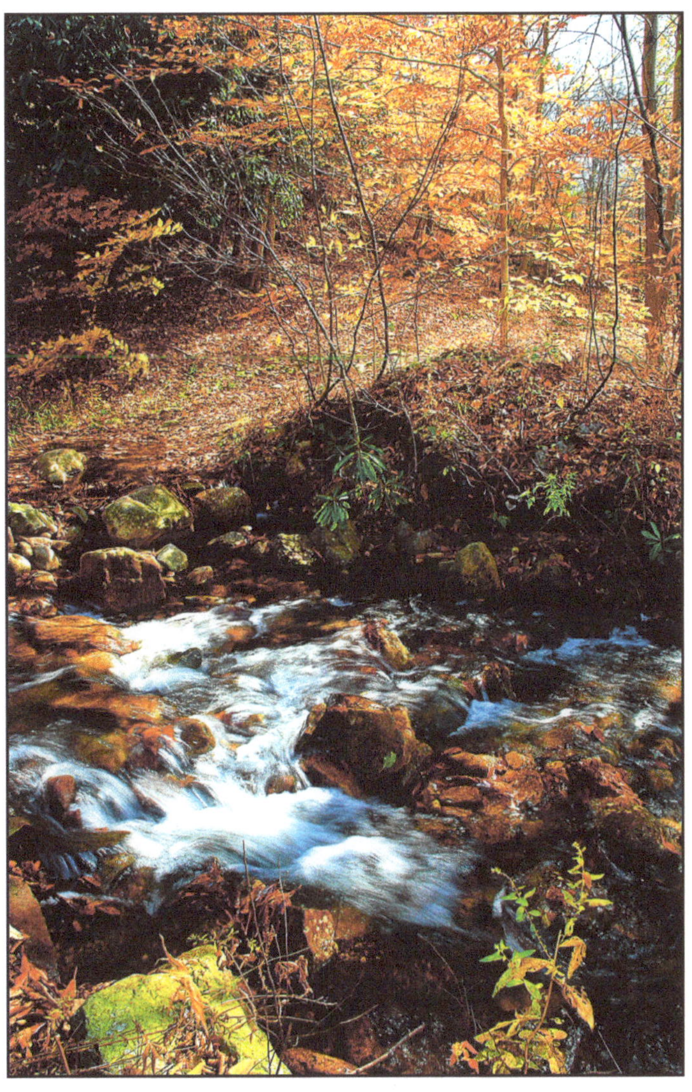

"To hold, as 't were, the mirror up to nature..."
_William Shakespeare, Hamlet. Act iii. Sc. 2

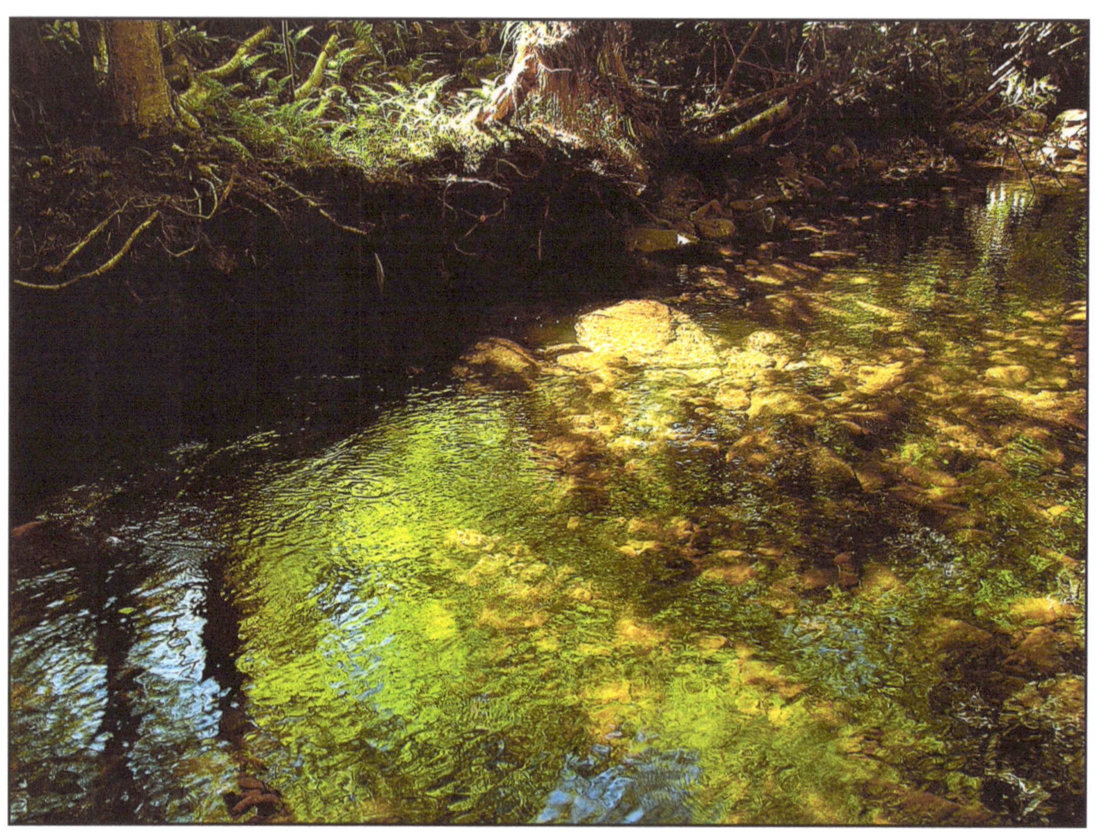

Albert Einstein, other scientists and philosophers, have been intrigued by the relationship between *time* and *light*. Small wonder. Consider, at the *speed of light*, about 186,000 miles per second, the time it takes sunlight to reflect from the banks of a stream, to the stream's surface, to the eyes of a nearby viewer, is *infinitesimal*. Yet in seeing the *reflection* of the banks in the stream, the viewer literally sees the *past*, albeit the very recent past!

Actually, when we *see* objects, we're really seeing the *light reflected from their surfaces*; when viewing transmitted light from distant stars, we may actually be seeing those stars as they appeared millions of years ago. Reflect upon that for a moment.

"By happy chance we saw
A twofold image: on a grassy bank
A snow-white ram, and in the crystal flood
Another and the same! "

_William Wordsworth

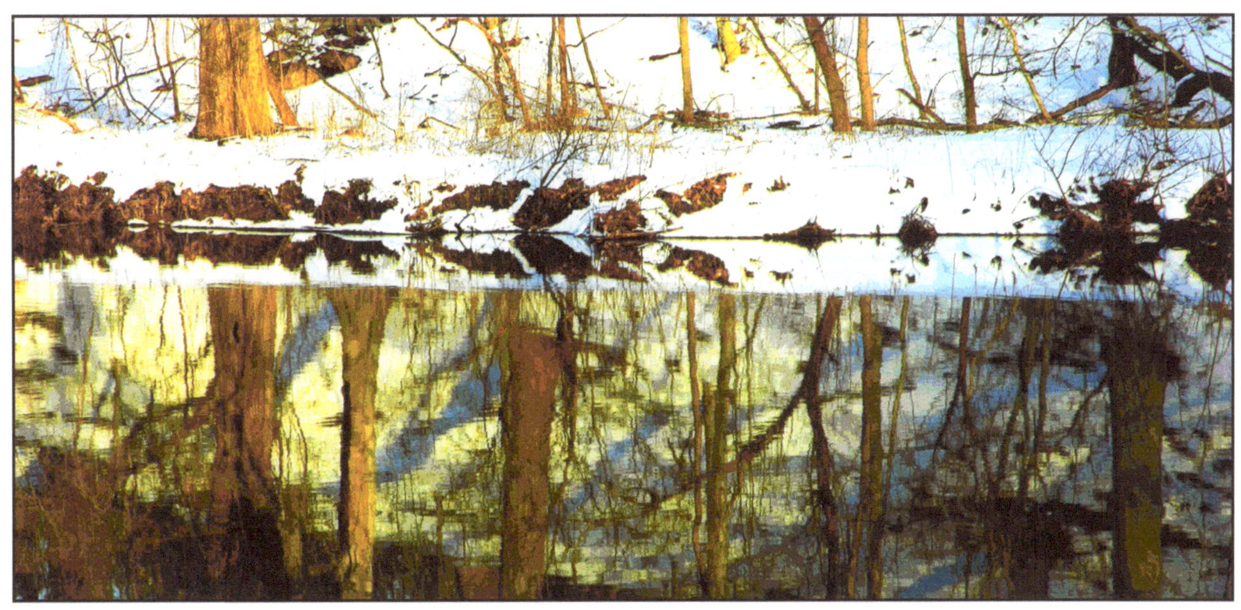

"Time is the image of eternity."

_Plato

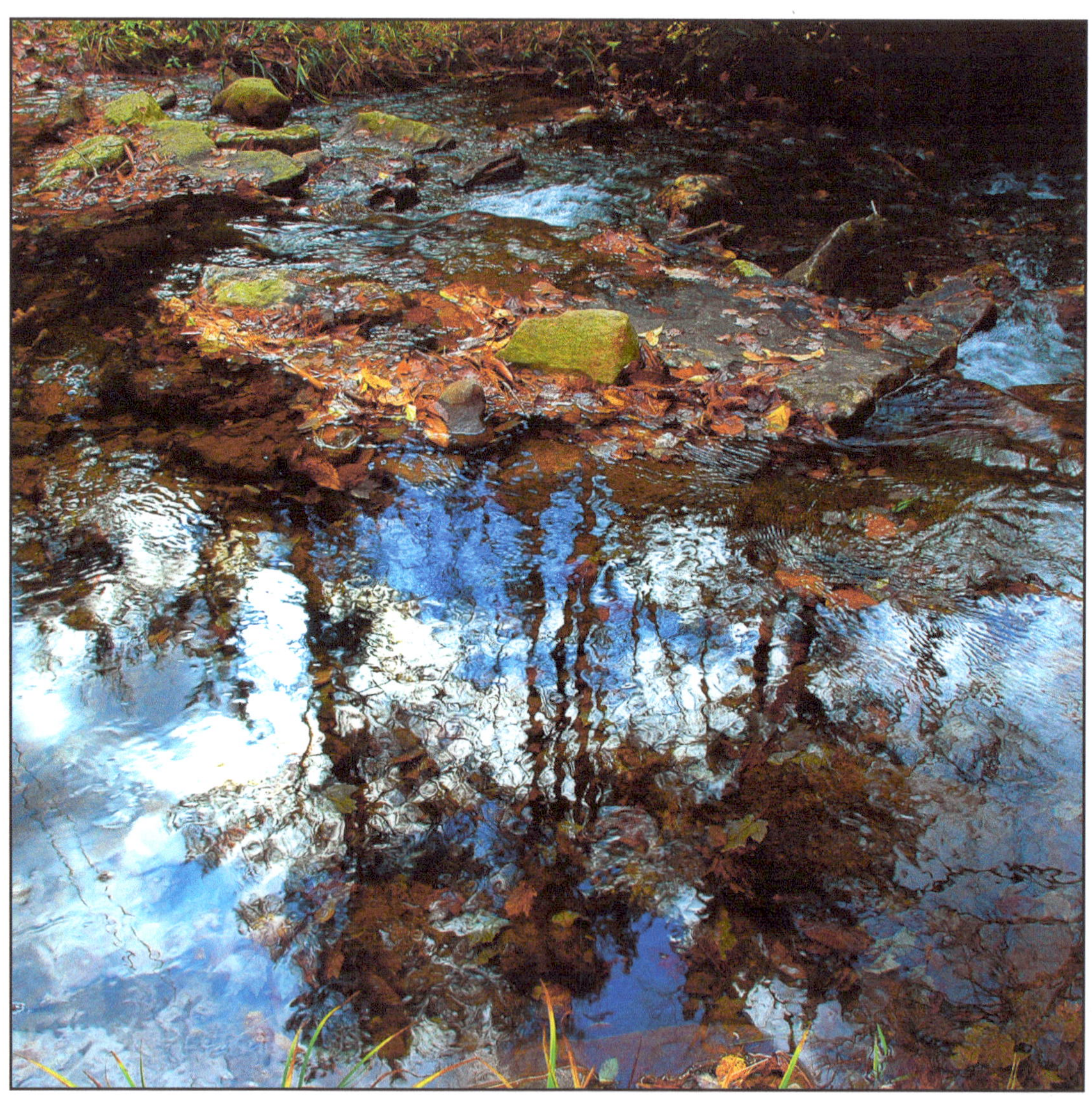

"Nature is the art of God."

_Sir Thomas Browne

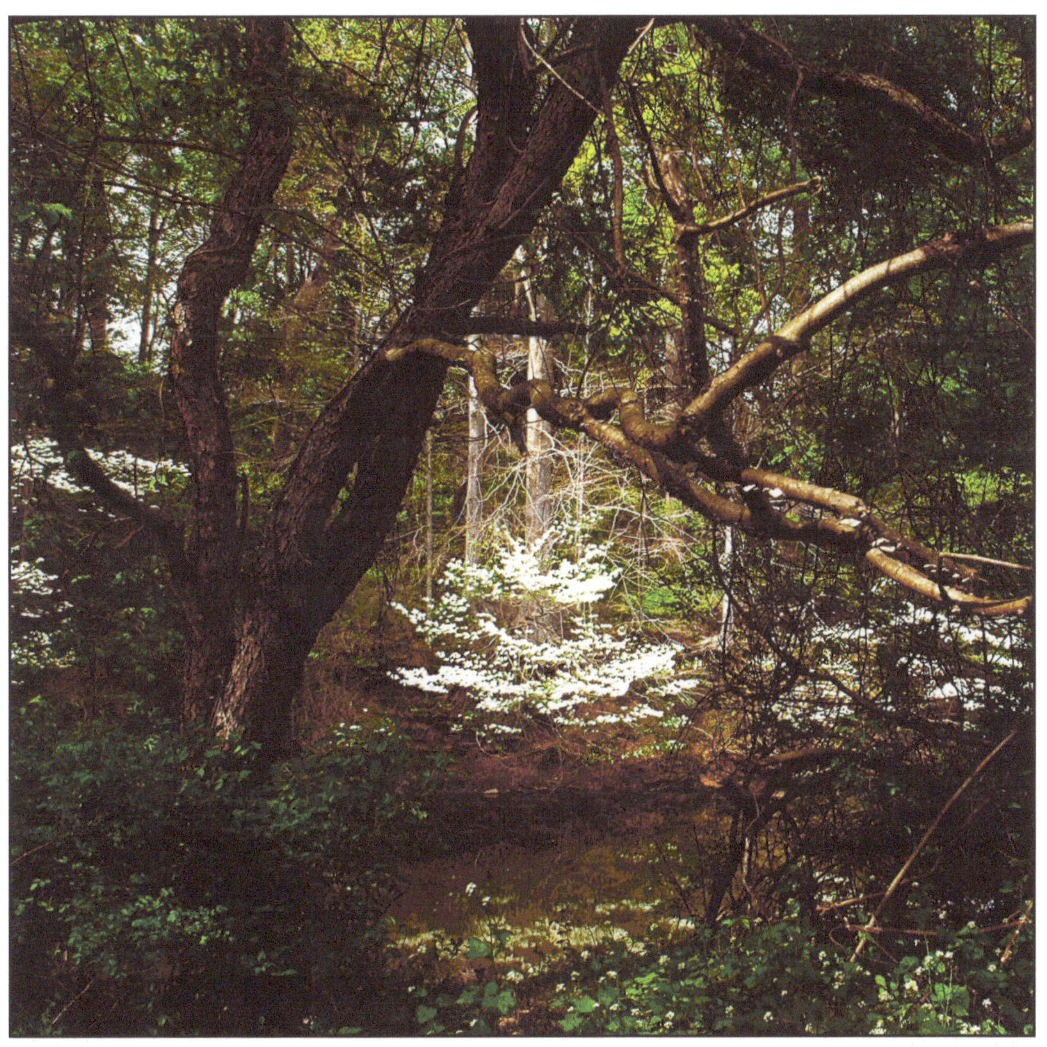

"Nature, exerting an unwearied power,
Forms, opens, and gives scent to every flower..."
_William Cowper

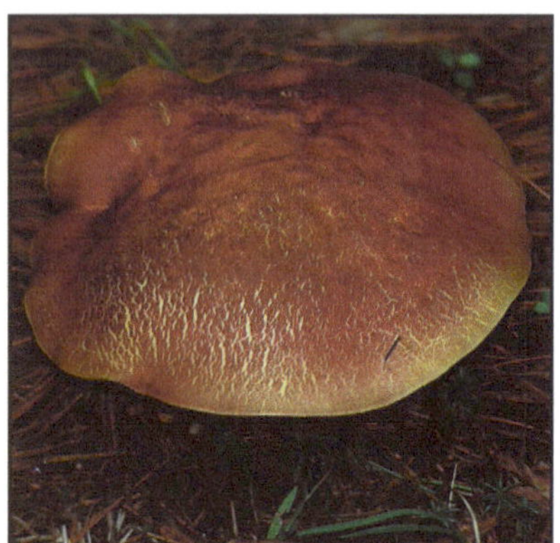

Bolete Mushroom
Genus Suillus

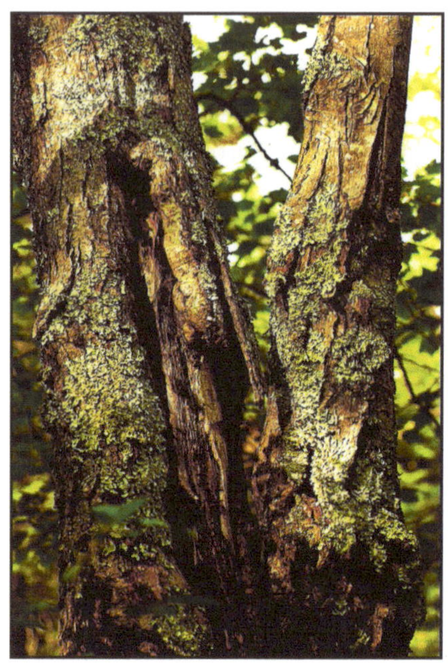

Cracked Shield Lichen (Parmelia sulcata) Growth on Hemlock Tree (Tsuga canadensis)

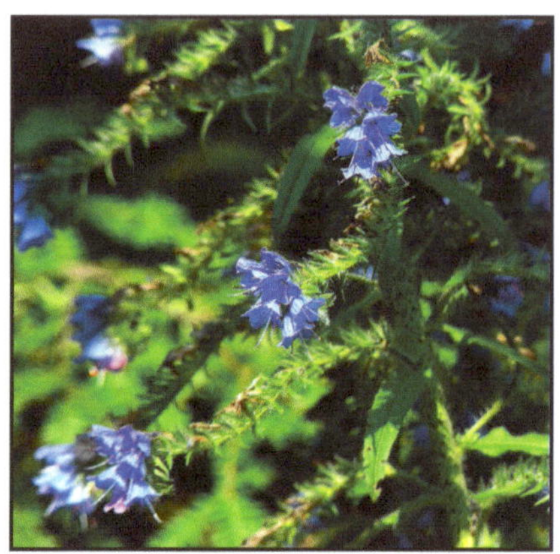

Blueweed
(Echium vulgare)

Biodiversity is essential to stream communities, a phenomenon that cannot be engineered by humans since it develops continuously over millions of years. The evolutionary development of biologically diverse forms is a complex process that advances by sucesses and mistakes. Some plant populations and species produce food and oxygen and maintain carbon dioxide levels while others decompose organic matter and return it to the environment. Some plant forms such as *Lichens*, can grow under the most adverse conditions and are actually *two* plants, an algae and a fungus, living inseparably as one, benefiting mutually.

"Everything in Nature contains all the powers of Nature. Everything is made of one hidden stuff."

_Ralph Waldo Emerson

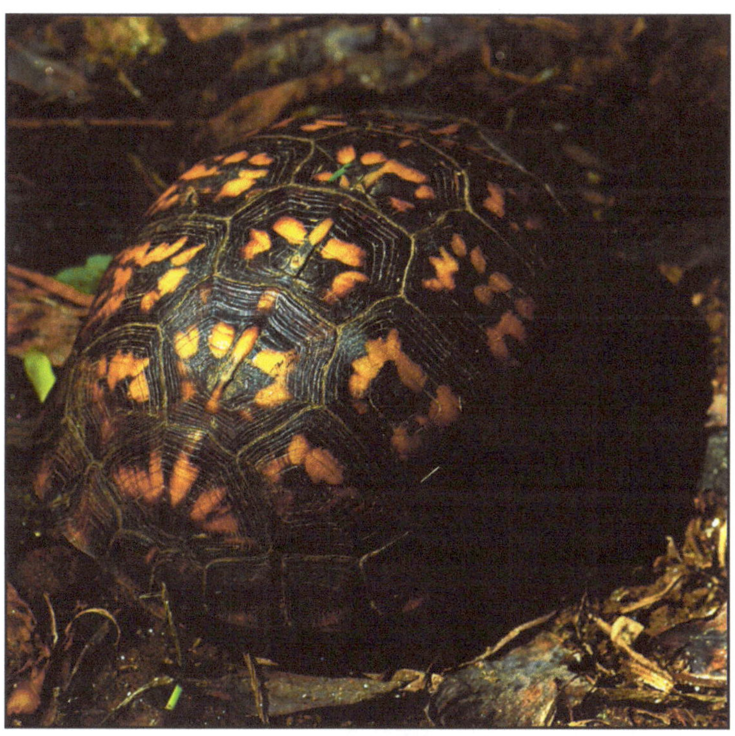

Eastern Box Turtle (Terrapene carolina)

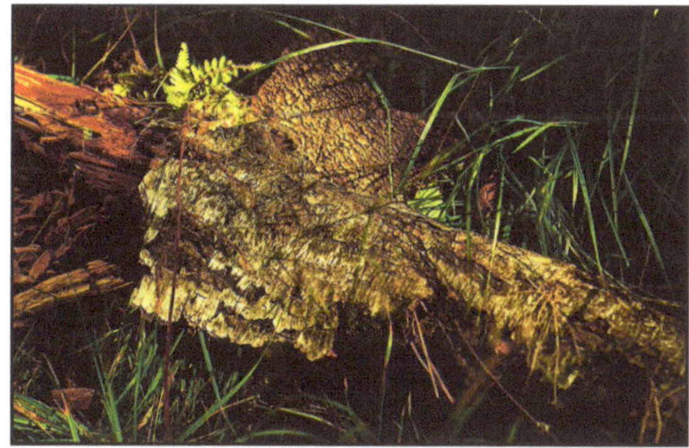

River Birch (Betula nigra) Torn Apart by a Black Bear (Ursa americana)

The Box Turtle, although a terrestrial reptile, oftens makes its living in damp forests near streams and floodplains. To its way of "thinking," when head, limbs and tail are inside the shell, it's *hidden* and safe.

The fallen Birch limb was ripped by a blacked bear in search of insects or grubs; while not in the picture, evidence of the bear's power, determination and hunger renders its existence in the area a fact, even while the bear itself, is *hidden*.

"For Art may err, but Nature cannot miss."

_John Dryden

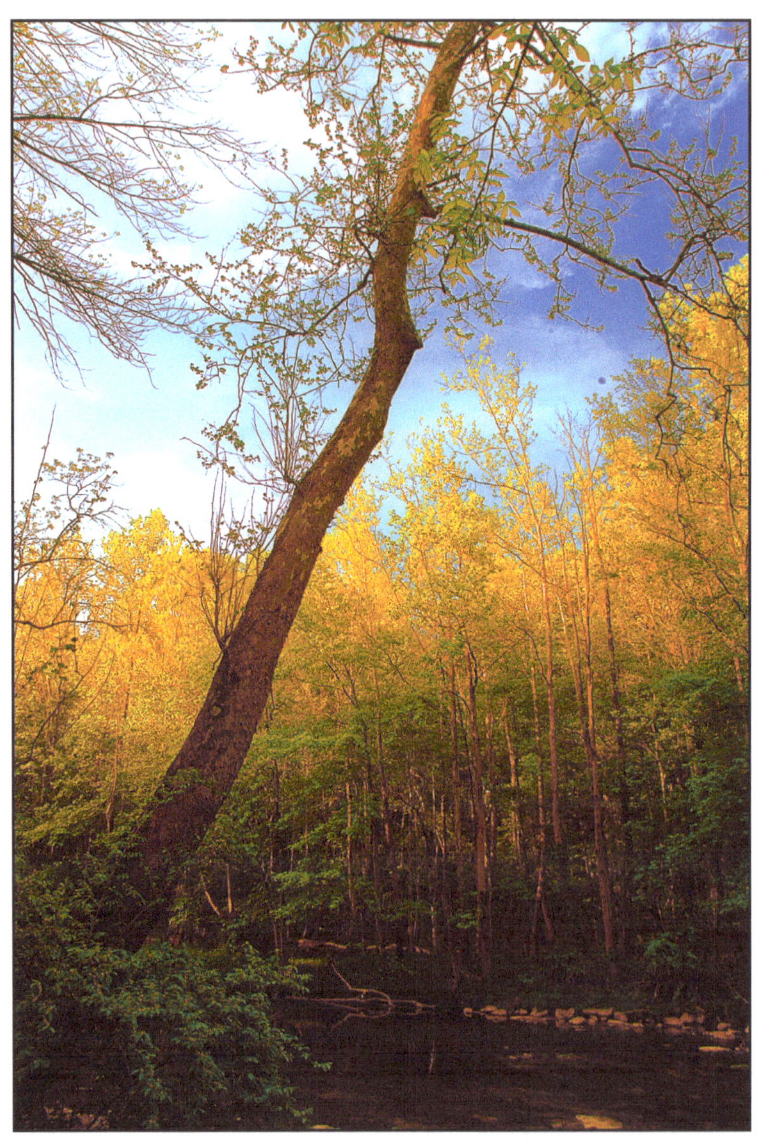

The Author

Arthur Gurmankin is former newspaper editor, technology consultant and professional educator. He has degrees in Biological Science and Fine Arts and currently does photography, digital art and oil painting along with producing books. In reverse chronological order, Arthur (or *Dude* as he is known to his grandchildren, Chase and Erika), is a grandfather, father and husband.

If not behind a camera or in front of a computer, you'll probably find the *Dude* around a stream in Pennsylvania's Pocono Mountains; if and when you do, he could be holding *both* a camera and a flyrod, perhaps in the act of photographing a brook trout which he's about to release. This behavior does not represent that of a person who is "indecisive," rather, someone who is twice as passionate as a normal person.

www.ingramcontent.com/pod-product-compliance
Lightning Source LLC
LaVergne TN
LVHW070154110826
845147LV00002B/401

* 9 7 8 0 6 1 5 1 6 9 7 5 0 *